Any Blonde Can Cook

Two Hundred 69 Ways To A Man's Heart

First Printing – September 2003

ISBN Number: 0-9744972-0-7

Library of Congress Control Number: 2003096764

Printed in the United States of America
TOOF COOKBOOK DIVISION

STARR ★ TOOF

670 South Cooper Street
Memphis, TN 38104

BLONDICATION

Any Blonde Can Cook: Two Hundred 69 Ways To a Man's Heart is our way of celebrating blondes in the kitchen. Whether you are born blonde, bottled blonde, act like a blonde, or just know and love a blonde, this cookbook is for you! If you are any of the above, chances are you have already experienced a "blonde moment," either first or secondhand. You don't have to be blonde to experience a blonde moment. In a way, **"we all share the same roots."** It just seems that as practicing blondes, we have more such moments than others. We want to **"blondicate"** this cookbook, not only to blondes, but to all the brunettes and redheads (regardless of their current hair color), who have helped inspire us to celebrate our roots and those special moments in the kitchen (not to mention their assistance with spelling, punctuation, and grammar). Thanks Peg!

A Blonde Moment In The Kitchen

Debbie, Anne and Cindy have had their share of Blonde Moments, many of them while cooking together. A typical such 'moment' occurred last Christmas. Debbie, a wonderful cook, was busy making an Italian Cream Cake from scratch. Her attentions that afternoon were divided among the difficult task at hand, preparing various other dishes that would precede the delectable dessert, and, most importantly, attempting to actively engage in the animated conversation occurring around the kitchen table. You see, Anne and Cindy had taken the opportunity to "assist" Debbie in the preparation of the magnificent meal. Their assistance took the form of sitting in her kitchen sipping fine wine, nibbling on a cheese ball, and running their mouths. It was a typical girlfriend afternoon.

Debbie, talking ninety miles an hour, laughing, and waving her arms in exaggerated animation, began to pour ingredients into a large bowl for the cake. First flour, then sugar and eggs, mixing and sifting along the way. An Italian Cream Cake from scratch has many ingredients. As Debbie cooked, the conversation and laughter grew louder and louder. Suddenly, Cindy noticed Debbie dump a can of creamed corn into the cake mixture. Puzzled, Cindy suffered her own blonde moment, and did not question Debbie's unusual choice of ingredients. Anne noticed as the second can of corn went in. Like Debbie and Cindy before her, she too suffered a blonde moment, started to say something, but got distracted when the phone rang.

As Debbie finished mixing the batter, she offered the dashers to her children. Italian Cream Cake batter is really divine. With eager anticipation, the children tasted the mixture. Immediately, soured expressions appeared on their faces. They both expressed immediate dislike. Cindy, still suffering a terminal case of "blonditis" casually spoke up and noted: "I've never seen anyone use creamed corn in their cake before."

The rest of the afternoon was spent adding various ingredients in an attempt to salvage the mixture as a corn pudding or casserole. It took three blondes to pull off this cooking blunder.

Blondes – you just gotta love 'em.

Everyone can use a little help in the kitchen no matter his or her hair color. So, we have put together an easy-to-follow compilation of recipes any blonde, brunette, or redhead can understand. These recipes, if properly followed, are sure to draw rave reviews, or to win any man's heart. Each recipe has been tried and tested with much love and laughter. Don't worry – the "Italian Cream Cake Corn Pudding" didn't make the cut. We really hope you have as much fun using this cookbook as we had making it. From our kitchen to yours, LOVE, LAUGH AND LIVE!

Debbie Thornton
Anne Walker
Cindy Lynch

Four Play

(Appetizers)

Four Play
(Appetizers)

Balls

Blonde Pick-Ups

Dips

Spreads

Q: Why can't a blonde make ice cubes?
A: They don't know the recipe.

Cocktail Balls

"Party Balls"

1 pound ground beef
1/2 cup breadcrumbs
1 egg
1 teaspoon salt
1 teaspoon pepper
2 Tablespoons ketchup
1 Tablespoon vinegar
1 Tablespoon soy sauce
1/4 teaspoon dry mustard

Combine first 5 ingredients and **form** into bite-size balls.
Brown balls in oven on 350 degrees for 10 minutes on each side.
Mix the last 4 ingredients together in saucepan on low.
Pour mixture and balls in crock pot and **simmer** on low for 1 hour.
Makes 40 balls.

Dried Beef Ball

"Hard Balls"

3 (8 ounce) cream cheese, softened
1 bunch green onions, finely chopped
1 (4 1/4 ounce) can chopped black olives
1 (7 ounce) can chopped mushrooms
2 (7 ounce) jars dried beef, finely chopped
3 teaspoons Accent seasoning

Mix all ingredients together.
Form into 2 or 3 balls.

Ham Ball

"Ham It Up Balls"

1/2 pound ham, ground
1/4 teaspoon curry powder
1/4 cup mayonnaise
1 (3 ounce) cream cheese, softened
1 Tablespoon milk
parsley to taste

Mix first 3 ingredients.
Shape into 1 ball.
Mix cream cheese, milk and **spread** on balls.
Roll in parsley and **chill**.

Olive Cheese Ball

"O Live A Little Balls"

16 ounces shredded sharp cheddar cheese
1 (8 ounce) cream cheese, softened
1/2 cup Spanish olives, finely chopped
1/2 teaspoon celery salt
1/2 teaspoon garlic salt
1/2 teaspoon Worcestershire

Mix all ingredients together.
Form into 2 or 3 balls.

Q: What does a blonde owl say?
A: "What, what?"

Preserves and Horseradish Ball

"Balls that Bite"

1 Tablespoon dry mustard
16 ounce pineapple/apricot preserves
1/2 of 10 ounce can of crushed pineapple
1 teaspoon pepper
1 (8 ounce) cream cheese, softened
1/4 cup prepared horseradish

Mix all ingredients together.
Form into 2 balls.

Pimiento Cheese Ball

"Red Eye Balls"

2 (16 ounce) shredded sharp cheddar cheese
1 (4 ounce) jar pimientos
1/2 bottle of Durkees dressing
2 cups mayonnaise
2 Tablespoons lemon juice
1 teaspoon mustard
1/3 teaspoon Worcestershire
1/2 teaspoon red pepper
1/2 teaspoon garlic salt

Mix all ingredients together.
Form into 2 balls.

Pineapple Ball

"Passionate Balls"

2 (8 ounce) cream cheese, softened
1 (8 ounce) can crushed pineapple, drained
1/4 cup bell pepper, finely chopped
2 Tablespoons minced onions
1 Tablespoon seasoned salt
2 cups pecans, finely chopped

Mix all ingredients together.
Form into 2 balls.

Salmon Ball

"Deannci Pink Balls"

1 (1 pound) can or 2 cups fresh salmon
1 (8 ounce) cream cheese, softened
1 Tablespoon lemon juice
2 teaspoons onions, finely chopped
1 teaspoon prepared horseradish
1/4 teaspoon salt
1/4 teaspoon liquid smoke
1/2 cup pecans, finely chopped
3 Tablespoons parsley

Drain and **flake** salmon.
Mix next 6 ingredients with salmon.
Chill for 1 hour, **form** into 1 ball.
Roll in pecans, parsley.

Sausage Balls
"Quick Balls"

10 ounces Coon cheese
1 pound pork sausage
3 cups Bisquick
1/4 teaspoon red pepper
1/4 teaspoon salt
1/4 teaspoon pepper

Melt cheese in microwave for 2-3 minutes or until melted. **Add** remainder of ingredients and **form** into bite-size balls. **Bake** at 350 degrees for 20-30 minutes.

Spinach Balls
"Mean Green Balls"

2 (10 ounce) packages frozen chopped spinach, cooked, drained
2 cups herb stuffing (not cubes)
1 onion, chopped
3 eggs, beaten
2 sticks margarine, softened
1/2 cup parmesan cheese
1 teaspoon thyme
1 teaspoon garlic salt
pepper to taste

Mix all ingredients together.
Form into bite-size balls.
Freeze on cookie sheet until hard.
Bake at 350 degrees for 15-20 minutes.

Artichoke Squares

"Seductive Squares"

2 (6 ounce) jars marinated artichokes
1/2 cup onion, finely chopped
1/2 teaspoon minced garlic
4 eggs, beaten
1/4 cup breadcrumbs
1/2 teaspoon hot sauce
1/2 teaspoon oregano
1/2 teaspoon salt & pepper
16 ounces shredded cheddar cheese

Drain juice from 1 jar of artichokes into skillet.
Sauté onion and garlic in juice.
Drain other jar and **chop** all artichokes.
Put artichokes in skillet.
Add next 6 ingredients in a separate bowl.
Combine all ingredients together.
Pour into a 9x13 baking dish.
Bake at 325 for 35-40 minutes.
Cut into squares.

Q: How do you drown a blonde?
A: Put a scratch-n-sniff sticker at the bottom of a pool.

Cheese Wafers

"Wacky Wafers"

- **2 sticks margarine, softened**
- **16 ounces shredded sharp cheddar cheese**
- **3 cups flour**
- **1/2 teaspoon dry mustard**
- **1/2 teaspoon salt**
- **1/2 teaspoon cayenne pepper**

Mix all ingredients together.
Form into bite-size balls and **press** down with a fork.
Place on cookie sheet.
Bake at 350 degrees for 15 minutes.

Dent Removal

A blonde left her car out in a hailstorm. When the storm was over she checked the car and found out it was covered with small dents. She went to the local garage and inquired how to fix the problem. The mechanic jokingly told her to blow on the tailpipe and the dents would be removed. So, she took the car home, parked it and proceeded to blow on the pipe. Another blonde came by and inquired what she was doing. She told her she was blowing on the tailpipe to remove the dents. The other blonde responded, "That's not going to work unless you roll up the window!"

Crab Rolls

"A Little Crabby"

1 (6 ounce) can crabmeat, rinsed, drained
1 (3 ounce) cream cheese, softened
2 (8 ounce) cans crescent rolls
1 egg yolk
1 teaspoon sesame seeds
1 (9 ounce) jar sweet & sour sauce

Combine crabmeat and cheese together.
Separate both cans of rolls.
Place 2 teaspoons of crab mixture on center of each roll.
Fold short ends of triangle over filling.
Pinch sides to seal and **roll** up.
Brush egg yolk over rolls.
Sprinkle with sesame seeds.
Place on cookie sheet.
Bake at 375 degrees for 15-20 minutes.
Serve with sweet and sour sauce.

Desert

A blonde, brunette and redhead are in a desert. The brunette says, "I brought some water so we don't get dehydrated." The redhead says, "I brought some suntan lotion so we don't get sunburned." Then the blonde says I brought a car door." The other girls said, "Why did you bring that?" Then the blonde says, "So I can roll down the window if it gets hot."

Nutty Crackers

"Sweet Trash"

- **1 (9 1/2 ounce) box Ritz Bitz peanut butter crackers**
- **1 cup dry roasted peanuts**
- **1/2 cup oil**
- **1 cup sugar**
- **1/2 cup karo syrup**
- **1 teaspoon vanilla extract**

Mix the first 2 ingredients.
Cook the next 4 ingredients in saucepan for 5 minutes.
Pour over crackers and peanuts.
Place on cookie sheet.
Bake at 250 degrees for 1 hour.
Stir every 20 minutes.

Oyster Crackers

"Crunchy Mullusks"

- **1 package dry Ranch buttermilk dressing mix**
- **1 cup oil**
- **1/2 teaspoon dried dill weed**
- **1/4 teaspoon garlic powder**
- **1/4 teaspoon lemon pepper**
- **1 (16 ounce) box plain oyster crackers**

Combine first 5 ingredients in order given.
Pour over cracker and **stir** to coat.
Place on cookie sheet.
Bake at 350 degrees for 15 minutes.

Mexican Squares

"Sleek Squares"

1	(4 1/2 ounce) can chopped green chilies
1	(15 ounce) can cream-style corn
1	(8 1/2 ounce) box corn muffin mix
1/2	onion, finely chopped
3	eggs, beaten
1 1/2	cups milk
1/2	cup oil
1/8	teaspoon salt
16	ounces shredded sharp cheddar cheese

Mix all ingredients together.
Pour into greased 9x13 baking dish.
Bake at 425 degrees for 25-30 minutes.

Bus Stop

Two blondes are waiting at a bus stop. When a bus pulls up and opens the door, one of the blondes leans inside and asks the bus driver: "Will this bus take me to 5th Avenue?"

The bus driver shakes his head and says, "No, I'm sorry."

At this, the other blonde leans inside, smiles, and twitters: "Will it take ME?"

Mushroom Snacks

"Mushy Bites"

2 (3 ounce) cream cheese, softened
1 (7 ounce) can mushrooms pieces and stems, finely chopped
1 (4 ounce) jar pimientos
2 Tablespoons Dijon mustard
2 (8 ounce) cans crescent rolls
2 eggs, beaten

Combine first 4 ingredients.
Separate rolls into 4 rectangles and **seal** perforations together.
Spread each rectangle with 1/4 of mushroom mixture.
Start with long side and **roll up**.
Cut each roll into 6 pieces and **place** seam side down.
Place on cookie sheet.
Brush with egg and **bake** at 375 degrees for 12 to 15 minutes.
Makes 50.

Q: What did the blonde get on her A.C.T.?
A: Nail polish!!!!!

Stuffed Mushrooms

"It's Stuffed"

25 mushrooms
1/2 stick margarine
1 small onion, finely chopped
8 ounces shredded mozzarella cheese
1 (3 ounce) jar bacon bits
3/4 cup breadcrumbs

Rinse mushrooms, **remove** stems.
Set caps aside.
Chop stems finely, **sauté** with onions in margarine.
Remove from heat, **stir** in last three ingredients.
Take mixture and **stuff** into caps.
Place on cookie sheet.
Bake at 350 for 30-35 minutes.

Blonde Cook

A blonde went to the doctor with burnt feet, "How did you do it?" asked the doctor .... "Cooking soup" .... The instructions said, "Open can .... stand in boiling water for 7 minutes."

Garden Pizza

"Veg-Out Pizza"

- **1 (8 ounce) can crescent rolls**
- **1 (8 ounce) cream cheese, softened**
- **1/3 cup mayonnaise**
- **1/4 teaspoon salt**
- **1 teaspoon dried dill weed**
- **1 teaspoon minced onions**
- **2 cups vegetables (of your choice) finely chopped**
- **1/2 cup green onions, finely chopped**
- **1/2 cup carrots, shredded**

Spread crescent rolls out on 12" round pizza pan.
Press all seams together.
Bake at 375 degrees for 10 minutes.
Blend next 5 ingredients together until smooth.
Spread on baked crust.
Mix together raw veggies, **sprinkle** over cream cheese mixture.
Top with green onions, carrots.
Chill until served.

Q: Why did the blonde stare at the frozen orange juice can for two hours?
A: Because it said "concentrate."

Shrimp Munchies

"Seductive Shrimp Snack"

1 (5 ounce) jar Old English cheese
1 stick margarine, softened
1 ($4^1/_2$ ounce) can tiny shrimp, drained, chopped
$^1/_2$ teaspoon garlic powder
1 teaspoon of hot sauce
5-6 halved English muffins

Mix first 5 ingredients.
Spread on muffins.
Freeze on cookie sheet for about 30 minutes.
Cut like a pizza in 8 bite-size pieces.
Bake at 350 degrees for 10-15 minutes.

Q: Why did the blonde keep a coat hanger in her back seat?
A: In case she locks the keys in her car.

Spinach Squares

"Sassy Squares"

- **$1/2$ stick margarine**
- **$1/2$ onion, finely chopped**
- **8 ounces fresh sliced mushrooms**
- **4 eggs, beaten**
- **$1/4$ cup breadcrumbs**
- **1 can cream of mushroom soup**
- **$1/4$ cup parmesan cheese**
- **$1/8$ teaspoon pepper, oregano, basil**
- **2 (10 ounce) packages chopped frozen spinach, thawed & well drained**

Sauté margarine with onions and mushrooms.
Combine rest of ingredients with onion and mushroom mixture.
Place in greased 9x13 baking dish.
Bake at 325 degrees for 20-25 minutes.
Cut into squares.

Disco Nights

There are 17 blondes standing outside a disco but they could not get in .... the sign said, "Must be 18 to enter."

Deep Dish Taco Squares

"Deep T"

- **1/2 pound ground beef**
- **1 Tablespoon onion, finely chopped**
- **1 cup Bisquick**
- **1/4 cup cold water**
- **2 tomatoes, chopped**
- **1 bell pepper, chopped**
- **1/2 cup sour cream**
- **1/3 cup mayonnaise**
- **4 ounces shredded cheddar cheese**

Grease 8x8 pan.
Brown ground beef and onion, then **drain**.
Mix Bisquick & water until dough forms.
Pat in pan, **pressing** 1/2 inch up sides.
Layer beef, tomatoes and green pepper in pan.
Mix last 3 ingredients together.
Spoon sour cream mixture over top of peppers.
Bake at 375 degrees 25-30 minutes.

Q: How does a blonde make instant pudding?
A: Places the box in the microwave and looks for the "instant pudding" setting.

Tomato Feta Tarts

"Finger Fetas"

1 (15 ounce) box piecrust (2 in a box)
1/2 (4 ounce) jar basil
4 Roma tomatoes, sliced
4 ounces feta cheese
olive oil
Cavendar's Greek Seasoning

Take a top off of a spice jar to use for a circle cutter.
Cut circles out of piecrust and **place** in mini muffin tins.
Bake 5 minutes and **remove** from muffin tins.
Place pie crust circles on cookie sheet.
Layer next 5 ingredients in order on pie circles.
Bake at 350 degrees for 15-20 minutes.

Mexican Tortilla

"Tingling Tortilla's"

6 (6-inch) flour tortillas
1 (15 ounce) can refried beans
1 red bell pepper, diced
1 green bell pepper, diced
1/2 cup taco sauce
8 ounces shredded Mexican cheese

Place tortillas on cookie sheet.
Bake at 400 degrees for 5 minutes.
Spread refried beans on each tortilla.
Top with peppers then taco sauce.
Sprinkle with cheese.
Bake at 325 degrees for 5-8 minutes.

Veggie Cream Cheese Sandwiches

"Dream Cream Sandwiches"

- **1 Tablespoon lemon juice**
- **1 (8 ounce) cream cheese, softened**
- **1 Tablespoon mayonnaise**
- **1/2 cup carrots, shredded**
- **1/4 cup bell pepper, grated**
- **1/2 cup cucumber, grated**
- **1/4 cup onion, finely chopped**
- **salt to taste**
- **pepper to taste**

Combine first 3 ingredients.
Add in rest of ingredients.
Chill and **serve** on bread.

Q: Why does the blonde throw breadcrumbs in the toilet every morning?
A: To feed the toilet duck!

Almond Scoring Dip

"He's All man"

1/3 cup almonds, sliced
2 (8 ounce) cream cheese, whipped
1 Tablespoon milk
1/4 teaspoon garlic powder
1/4 teaspoon onion powder
1/4 teaspoon oregano
1/8 teaspoon basil
1/8 teaspoon salt
1/8 teaspoon pepper

Spread almonds on sheet.
Bake at 350 degrees for 5-10 minutes.
Mix all ingredients together except almonds.
Mix in almonds just before serving.
Serve with crackers.

Q: Why do blondes drive BMWs?
A: Because they can spell it.

Hot Asparagus Dip

"Hot Aspirations"

- **2 (12 ounce) cans cut asparagus spears, drained**
- **1 1/2 cups mayonnaise**
- **1/2 cup sour cream**
- **1 1/2 cups parmesan cheese**
- **1/8 teaspoon minced garlic**
- **1/8 teaspoon hot sauce**

Mash asparagus.
Combine all ingredients together.
Pour in 8x8 baking dish.
Bake at 350 degrees for 20-30 minutes.
Serve with corn chips.

Artichoke Cheese Dip

"Don't Choke"

- **16 ounces shredded mozzarella cheese**
- **1 cup parmesan cheese**
- **1 cup mayonnaise**
- **1 (16 ounce) can artichoke hearts, drained, chopped**
- **1 red pepper, finely chopped**
- **1 teaspoon minced garlic**

Mix all ingredients together.
Cook at 250 degrees for 1 hour in oven or crockpot.
Serve with crackers.

Crab Dip

"Don't Be Crabby"

1 Tablespoon lemon juice
1 Tablespoon Worcestershire
1 Tablespoon onion, finely chopped
2 (8 ounce) cream cheese, softened
3 Tablespoons mayonnaise
1 (12 ounce) bottle chili sauce
1/2 pound fresh crabmeat or 1 (6 ounce) can
8 ounces shredded mozzarella cheese
parsley flakes

This dip is layered.
Mix first 5 ingredients for first layer.
Spread chili sauce as second layer.
Spread crabmeat as third layer.
Spread cheese as fourth layer.
Sprinkle with parsley flakes.
Serve with crackers.

Crawfish Dip

"Don't Crawfish Me"

2 cups crawfish, cooked, chopped
1 (8 ounce) sour cream
1 (8 ounce) cream cheese, softened
1/2 cup celery, finely chopped
1/2 cup onion, finely chopped
1 teaspoon seafood seasoning

Mix all ingredients together.
Serve with crackers.

Curry Dip

"Golden Blonde"

- **1½ cups mayonnaise**
- **2 teaspoons curry powder**
- **1 Tablespoon onion, finely chopped**
- **½ teaspoon dry mustard**
- **½ teaspoon salt and pepper**
- **dash of hot sauce**

Mix all ingredients together.
Better if **made** a day ahead of time.
Serve with raw vegetables.

Fruit Dip

"Ditzy Deannci"

- **1 (8 ounce) cream cheese, softened**
- **2 teaspoons milk**
- **2 Tablespoons brown sugar**
- **1 teaspoon cinnamon**
- **1 teaspoon vanilla extract**
- **¼ teaspoon nutmeg**

Mix all ingredients together.
Serve with fruit.

Monterey Jack Salsa Dip

"Slip Out The Back Jack"

- **1 tomato, chopped**
- **1 bunch green onions, chopped**
- **1 (4 1/4 ounce) can chopped black olives**
- **1 (4 1/2 ounce) can chopped green chilies**
- **1/2 cup Italian dressing**
- **8 ounces shredded Monterey Jack cheese**

Mix all ingredients together.
Serve with chips.

Pumpkin Dip

"My Little Punkin"

- **2 (8 ounce) cream cheese, softened**
- **2 (16 ounce) boxes powdered sugar**
- **1 (15 ounce) can pumpkin**
- **2 teaspoons cinnamon**
- **1 teaspoon sugar**
- **1 teaspoon ginger**

Mix all ingredients together.
Serve with ginger snaps.

Q: What do you call 24 blondes in a cardboard box?
A: A case of empties.

Shrimp Dip

"Shrunken Shrimp"

2 (8 ounce) cream cheese, softened
2/3 cup milk
4 teaspoons onions, finely chopped
4 teaspoons lemon juice
dash of Worcestershire
2 (4 1/2 ounce) cans shrimp, drained

Mix all ingredients in order.
Chill at least 6 hours.
Serve with chips or crackers.

Hot Sombrero Dip

"Hottie Tottie"

1 pound ground beef, cooked, drained
2 (14 1/2 ounce) cans bean dip
1 (4 1/2 ounce) can chopped green chilies
1 (8 ounce) jar picante sauce
8 ounces shredded cheddar cheese
2 tomatoes, chopped

This dip is layered.
Mix first 5 ingredients in order.
Pour in 9x13 baking dish.
Bake at 375 degrees until cheese is melted.
Sprinkle with tomatoes.
Serve with chips.

Hot Spinach Dip

"Popeye's Passion"

- **2 (10 ounce) packages frozen chopped spinach**
- **1/2 cup onion, finely chopped**
- **1 pickled jalapeño, finely chopped**
- **1 (8 ounce) cream cheese, softened**
- **16 ounces shredded Monterey Jack cheese**
- **1/3 cup half & half cream**
- **1 teaspoon hot sauce**
- **1 (10 ounce) can Rotel tomatoes, diced**
- **2 tomatoes, chopped**

Thaw spinach, **press** excess moisture out.
Combine all ingredients together except tomatoes.
Pour in 9x13 baking dish.
Bake at 350 degrees for 25-30 minutes.
Sprinkle with fresh tomatoes.

Q: What do you call a brunette with a blonde on either side?
A: An interpreter.

Hot Tamale Dip

"Hot Flash"

1 (15 ounce) can chili without beans
12 canned or homemade hot tamales
1 (15 1/4 ounce) can whole corn, drained
1 (4 1/4 ounce) can chopped black olives
1 (15 ounce) bag of Fritos
1/2 cup shredded cheddar cheese

Mash chili and tamales together.
Add corn and black olives to tamale mixture.
Place in 9x13 baking dish.
Top with Fritos and cheese.
Bake at 350 degrees until bubbly.

Vidalia Onion Dip

"Kissable Onion"

3 Vidalia onions, chopped
2 Tablespoons margarine
1/2 teaspoon minced garlic
1 cup mayonnaise
8 ounces shredded sharp cheddar cheese
1/2 teaspoon hot sauce

Sauté onion in margarine.
Blend all ingredients together.
Pour in 9x13 baking dish.
Bake at 375 degrees 20-25 minutes.

Water Chestnut Dip

"Chest and Nuts"

1 (8 ounce) sour cream
1 cup mayonnaise
1 bunch green onions, finely chopped
1 (8 ounce) can water chestnuts, chopped
½ teaspoon soy sauce
½ teaspoon hot sauce

Mix all ingredients together.
Serve with crackers or chips.

3 Cheese Spread

"3-Way Spread"

1 (5 ounce) jar bleu cheese
1 (5 ounce) jar Old English cheese
2 (8 ounce) cream cheese, softened
1 cup pecans, chopped
1 teaspoon Worcestershire
2 Tablespoons onion flakes

Mix all ingredients together.
Serve with crackers.

Artichoke Spread

"Alluring Spread"

- **1 (14 ounce) can artichoke hearts, drained**
- **5 green onions, finely chopped**
- **1 Tablespoon mayonnaise**
- **1 teaspoon lemon juice**
- **1/8 teaspoon salt**
- **1/8 teaspoon pepper**

Mash artichoke hearts to pulp.
Mix rest of ingredients in order.
Serve with crackers.

Chicken Spread

"Chick's Spread"

- **2 chicken breasts, cooked and chopped**
- **1 (8 ounce) cream cheese, softened**
- **1/3 cup steak sauce**
- **1/3 cup celery, chopped**
- **1 teaspoon dill weed**
- **1 teaspoon lemon pepper**

Mix all ingredients together.
Serve on bread or crackers

Crab Spread

"Creamy Crab Spread"

1/2 pound lump crabmeat or 6 ounce can
1 (8 ounce) cream cheese, softened
1 teaspoon Worcestershire
1 teaspoon minced chives
1 teaspoon parsley
1/2 teaspoon Old Bay seasoning

Drain crabmeat, **removing** any bits.
Combine remaining ingredients.
Cover and **chill** 8 hours.
Serve with crackers.

Cranberry Cheese Spread

"Ruby Red Spread"

1 (16 ounce) can whole cranberry sauce
1 (4 1/2 ounce) can diced green chilies
2 Tablespoons green onions, sliced
1 Tablespoon lime juice
1 teaspoon garlic powder
1/2 teaspoon garlic salt
1/2 teaspoon cayenne pepper
1/2 teaspoon chili powder
1 (8 ounce) cream cheese

Mix first 8 ingredients together.
Spoon 1 cup cranberry mixture over cream cheese.
Serve with crackers.

Black Olive Spread

"Bodacious Black Spread"

- **$^1/_2$ cup pecans, finely chopped**
- **1 ($4^1/_4$ ounce) can chopped black olives**
- **1 (8 ounce) cream cheese, softened**
- **$^1/_2$ teaspoon Worcestershire**
- **$^1/_8$ teaspoon seasoned salt**
- **$^1/_2$ teaspoon lemon juice**

Mix all ingredients together.
Serve on bread or crackers.

Nut-Olive Spread

"The Big "O" Spread"

- **1 (8 ounce) cream cheese, softened**
- **$^1/_2$ cup mayonnaise**
- **2 Tablespoons olive juice**
- **$^1/_2$ teaspoon red pepper**
- **$^3/_4$ cup pecans, chopped**
- **$1^1/_2$ cups salad olives, chopped**

Mix all ingredients together.
Serve on bread or crackers.

Q: Why did the blonde put lipstick on her forehead?
A: Trying to make up her mind.

Salmon Spread
"Sookie Spread"

1 (4 ounce) can smoked salmon
3 green onions, finely chopped
1 (8 ounce) cream cheese, softened
1 teaspoon lemon juice
2 teaspoons prepared horseradish
1/8 teaspoon salt

Mix all ingredients together.
Serve with crackers.

Shrimp Spread
"Sexy Spread"

1 (3 ounce) cream cheese, softened
1 (8 ounce) sour cream
2 teaspoons lemon juice
1 package dry Italian dressing mix
1 (4 1/4 ounce) can shrimp, rinsed, drained
1/8 teaspoon pepper

Mix all ingredients together.
Serve with crackers.

Tex-Mex Spread

"Cowboy Spread"

1 (8 ounce) cream cheese, softened
1 (8 ounce) sour cream
2 (8 ounce) jars taco sauce
1 bunch green onions, chopped
2 ($4^1/_4$ ounce) cans chopped black olives
2 tomatoes, chopped

Mix first 2 ingredients together.
Spread on a pizza pan.
Pour taco sauce over cream cheese mixture.
Sprinkle next 3 ingredients over taco sauce.
Serve with chips.

Blonde in the Sun

A Russian, an American, and a Blonde were talking one day. The Russian said, "We were the first in space!" The American said, "We were the first on the moon!" The Blonde said, "So what. We're going to be the first on the sun!" The Russian and the American looked at each other and shook their heads. "You can't land on the sun, you idiot! You'll burn up!" said the Russian. To which the Blonde replied, "We're not stupid, you know. We're going at night!"

A.M. Spirits

(Beverages, Breads & Breakfast Fixins)

A.M. Spirits
(Beverages, Breads, Breakfast Fixins)

Beverages

Breads

Breakfast Fixins

Iced Coffee

"Muddy Rivers"

1 quart vanilla ice cream, softened
1/4 cup sugar
3/4 teaspoon nutmeg
3 cups milk
1 teaspoon vanilla extract
8 cups brewed coffee, room temperature

Mix all ingredients together in punch bowl.

Parker House Chocolate Martini

"Deannci's Favorite"

1 Tablespoon sugar
1 Tablespoon cocoa
1 1/2 ounces premium vodka
1/2 ounce dark crème de cacao liqueur
1/2 ounce dark chocolate liqueur
3 chocolate chips

Chill martini glass.
Mix equal parts of sugar and cocoa.
Dip rim of martini glass into cocoa mixture.
Mix next 3 ingredients together with ice in metal shaker.
Shake vigorously and **strain** ice.
Pour into martini glass.
Drop chocolate chips in bottom.

Martini Slush

"Deannci's Cosmo"

- **1 (6 ounce) can frozen orange juice**
- **1 (6 ounce) can frozen lemonade**
- **1 (6 ounce) can frozen limeade**
- **½ cup sugar**
- **1 cup vodka**
- **2 cans of water**

Mix all ingredients together.
Pour 2 cups of mixture into blender with ice.

Lemon Punch

"Blonde Slush"

- **2 (3 ounce) boxes lemon jello**
- **1 cup boiling water**
- **2 cups sugar**
- **8 cups cold water**
- **1 (46 ounce) can pineapple juice**
- **1 (2 liter) 7-Up**

Dissolve jello in boiling water.
Mix all ingredients together except 7-Up.
Freeze for 2 hours.
Add 7-Up when ready to serve.
Pour into punch bowl.

Spring Time Punch

"Special Touch Punch"

$2^1/_2$ cups water
2 cups sugar
1 cup lemon juice
1 cup orange juice
1 cup pineapple juice
2 quarts ginger ale

Bring sugar and water to a boil for 10 minutes.
Remove from heat.
Stir in lemon, orange and pineapple juices.
Refrigerate.
Before serving, **add** ginger ale.
Makes 3 quarts.

Strawberry Punch

"Strawberry Blonde Punch"

3 (3 ounce) boxes strawberry jello
4 cups hot water
4 cups sugar
9 cups cold water
1 (46 ounce) can pineapple juice
1 (6 ounce) can frozen orange juice
2 (6 ounce) cans frozen lemonade
3 (10 ounce) bottles club soda
1 (10 ounce) box frozen strawberries, thawed

Dissolve jello in hot water.
Combine all ingredients in punch bowl.

Sangria

"Blonde Sangria"

1 fifth dry white wine
1 cup unsweetened pineapple juice
1/3 cup orange juice
3 Tablespoons lemon juice
1 Tablespoon lime juice
1/4 cup sugar
12 ounces Sprite
pineapple chunks
orange slices

Mix first 6 ingredients together and **chill**.
Add sprite and fruits when ready to serve.

Almond Tea

"Enhance Vance"

1/2 cup lemon flavored Lipton Instant Tea Mix
16 cups hot water, divided
1 cup sugar
1 (12 ounce) can frozen lemonade
2 Tablespoons almond extract
2 teaspoons vanilla extract

Dissolve tea mix into 4 cups of hot water in saucepan on medium heat.
Add sugar and 4 more cups of water.
Boil 5 minutes.
Add 8 cups water, lemonade, almond and vanilla extract.
Boil for 3 minutes.
Serve over ice.

Juicy Tea

"Lip Smacker Tea"

1 cup instant sweetened tea mix
1 (6 ounce) can frozen limeade
1 (6 ounce) can frozen lemonade
1 (6 ounce) can frozen pineapple juice
2 cups cranberry juice
8 cups of water

Combine all ingredients together.

Mint Tea

"Meant-To-Be Tea"

7 tea bags, regular size
12 sprigs of mint
3 lemon rinds
8 cups boiling water
7 lemons, juiced
2 cups sugar

Steep tea, mint and lemon rinds for 15 minutes in water. **Remove** from water, **add** lemon juice and sugar.

Q: Why did the blonde get so excited after she finished her jigsaw puzzle in only six months?
A: Because on the box it said, "From 2-4 years."

Banana Bread

"Blondes Go Bananas"

- **1/2 cup oil**
- **1 cup sugar**
- **2 eggs**
- **1 cup all-purpose flour**
- **1 teaspoon baking soda**
- **1/2 teaspoon salt**
- **2-3 bananas, mashed**
- **2 teaspoons vanilla extract**
- **1/2 cup pecans, chopped**

Cream oil & sugar until light and fluffy.
Add eggs one at a time, **beating** well.
Sift together flour, baking soda & salt.
Add to creamed mixture.
Mix well.
Fold in bananas, vanilla & pecans.
Pour into greased loaf pan.
Bake at 350 degrees for 45 minutes.
Cool in pan for 10 minutes.

River Walk

There's this blonde out for a walk. She comes to a river and sees another blonde on the opposite bank. "Yoo –hoo!" She shouts, "How can I get to the other side?" The second blonde looks up the river then down the river and shouts back, "You ARE on the other side."

Bran Bread

"Always Ready"

- **1/2 box bran flakes**
- **1/2 cup oil**
- **2 cups buttermilk**
- **2 eggs, beaten**
- **2 1/2 cups self-rising flour**
- **1 1/2 cups sugar**

Combine all ingredients together.
Pour in well-greased loaf pan.
Bake at 350 degrees for 30-40 minutes.

Chocolate Macadamia Bread

"PMS Dough"

- **2 ounces unsweetened chocolate**
- **2 cups self-rising flour**
- **1 1/4 cups sugar**
- **1/3 cup oil**
- **2 eggs**
- **2 teaspoons vanilla extract**
- **1 teaspoon almond extract**
- **1 1/4 cups buttermilk**
- **1/2 cup macadamia nuts, finely chopped**

Melt chocolate in a double boiler on stove and **set** aside.
Mix all ingredients together in order.
Pour into greased loaf pan.
Bake at 350 degrees for 45 minutes.

Stuffed French Bread

"She's Stuffed"

1 loaf French bread
1 (8 ounce) sour cream
16 ounces shredded cheddar cheese
1/2 cup ham, chopped
1 bell pepper, chopped
1 teaspoon steak sauce

Hull out loaf of bread.
Combine all ingredients, including crumbs from bread.
Spoon back into loaf of bread.
Wrap in aluminum foil.
Bake at 350 degrees for 1 hour.
Serve as a side dish or with frito chips.

Q: What did the blonde say when she looked into a box of Cheerios?
A: "Oh look! Donut seeds!"

Mexican Corn Bread

"Jumpin Jack Flash"

- **2 eggs**
- **1 (15 ounce) can cream-style corn**
- **2/3 cup oil**
- **1 1/2 cups corn meal**
- **3 teaspoons baking powder**
- **1 Tablespoon salt**
- **2 jarred whole jalapeño peppers, chopped**
- **2 Tablespoons green onions, chopped**
- **8 ounces shredded cheddar cheese**

Mix first 8 ingredients together.
Pour half of the mixture into hot, well-greased skillet.
Sprinkle half of the cheese over the batter.
Add remaining corn meal mixture and **top** with the rest of the cheese.
Bake at 350 degrees for 1 hour.

Q: How do you hit a blonde and she would never know it?
A: With a thought!

Monkey Bread

"Let's Monkey Around"

- **3/4 cup sugar**
- **1 teaspoon cinnamon**
- **4 cans of 10 count biscuits**

GLAZE:

- **1 1/2 sticks margarine**
- **1 cup sugar**
- **2 teaspoons cinnamon**

Melt glaze ingredients together, **set** aside.
Mix sugar and cinnamon together.
Cut biscuits in quarters.
Roll in cinnamon-sugar mixture.
Place in a well-greased bundt pan.
Pour glaze mixture over top.
Bake at 350 degrees for 40 minutes or until bubbly.

Q: How do you make a blonde laugh on Monday mornings?
A: Tell them a joke on Friday night!

Parmesan Pull-Aparts

"Can't Pull Em Apart"

3 Tablespoons margarine
1 teaspoon dill seed
1 teaspoon poppy seed
1/4 teaspoon celery seed
1 (10 count) can flaky biscuits
1/4 cup parmesan cheese

Melt margarine in round cake pan.
Sprinkle all seeds in margarine.
Cut each biscuit into quarters.
Shake with parmesan cheese in a bag.
Place biscuits in cake pan.
Bake at 400 degrees for 15-18 minutes.

Pina Colada Bread

"Hawaiian Fling"

1 box pineapple cake mix
2 eggs
1/2 cup oil
1 cup water
1 cup coconut
1 cup pecans, chopped

Mix all ingredients together.
Pour into 2 loaf pans.
Bake at 350 degrees for 25-30 minutes.

Poppy Seed Bread

"Make His Eyes Pop"

- **$2^1/_2$ cups sugar**
- **$1^1/_3$ cups oil**
- **$1^1/_2$ cups milk**
- **3 eggs**
- **3 cups self-rising flour**
- **$1^1/_2$ Tablespoons poppy seed**
- **$1^1/_2$ teaspoons vanilla extract**
- **$1^1/_2$ teaspoons almond extract**

Mix all ingredients together in order listed.
Place into 2 well-greased loaf pans.
Bake at 325 degrees for 1 hour.

Strawberry Bread

"Strawberry Blonde"

- **3 cups self-rising flour**
- **2 cups sugar**
- **2 (10 ounce) packages frozen strawberries, reserve $^1/_2$ cup juice for spread**
- **1 cup oil**
- **4 eggs, beaten**
- **1 (8 ounce) cream cheese, softened**

Mix all ingredients, except strawberry juice and cream cheese.
Pour batter into 2 well-greased loaf pans.
Bake at 325 degrees for 1 hour.
Blend cream cheese with reserved strawberry juice.
Spread on loaves of bread.

Apple Dumplings

"Darling Dumpling"

1 (10 count) can biscuits
6 apples, peeled, chopped
1 (12 ounce) can 7-Up
1 cup sugar
1 stick margarine
1½ teaspoons cinnamon

Roll out each biscuit thinly.
Spoon equal amount of chopped apple on each biscuit.
Fold up to enclose apples, **crimping** edges to seal.
Place in 9x13 dish.
Combine remaining ingredients in saucepan.
Boil for 2 minutes and **pour** over dumplings.
Bake at 325 degrees for 30 minutes.

Knitting

A highway patrolman pulled alongside a speeding car on the freeway. Glancing at the car, he was astounded to see the blonde behind the wheel was knitting! Realizing that she was oblivious to his flashing lights and siren, the trooper cranked down his window, turned on his bullhorn and yelled, "PULL OVER!" "NO!" the blonde yelled back, "IT'S A SCARF!"

Breakfast Casserole
"While You Were Sleeping"

- **6 slices bread**
- **1/2 stick margarine, softened**
- **1 pound sausage, cooked, drained, crumbled**
- **8 ounces shredded sharp cheddar cheese**
- **5 eggs, beaten**
- **2 cups half & half cream**
- **1 teaspoon salt**
- **1 teaspoon dry mustard**
- **1/2 teaspoon pepper**

Spread butter on bread and **cut** into cubes.
Place in 9x13 baking dish.
Sprinkle cooked sausage over bread cubes.
Top with cheese.
Combine remaining ingredients.
Beat well and **pour** mixture over cheese.
Chill for at least 8 hours or overnight.
Bake at 350 degrees for 40-50 minutes.

Q: How do you drive a blonde crazy?
A: Give her a bag of M&Ms and tell her to alphabetize them.

Breakfast Pizza

"Breakfast in the Round"

- **2 (8 ounce) cans crescent rolls**
- **1 pound pork sausage, browned, drained**
- **1 cup frozen hash brown potatoes**
- **1 cup shredded sharp cheddar cheese**
- **4 eggs, beaten**
- **$^1/_2$ cup milk**

Place rolls on greased pizza pan placing pointed ends of crescents to center of pan, like pizza slices.
Spoon next 3 ingredients on rolls.
Beat eggs, milk and **pour** on top.
Bake at 375 degrees for 25 minutes.

Breakfast Tacos

"Payne Pork"

- **1 pound sausage**
- **1 (4$^1/_2$ ounce) can chopped green chilies**
- **12 eggs, beaten**
- **1 bunch green onions, chopped**
- **8 ounces shredded cheddar cheese**
- **10 flour tortillas**

Brown sausage and **drain**.
Beat eggs with chilies and **pour** over sausage
Sprinkle green onions over mixture and **mix** together.
Cook over medium heat until eggs are scrambled.
Sprinkle cheese over mixture.
Put mixture in tortillas and **wrap**.

Green Chilies & Sausage Casserole

"Self-Rising Pork"

- **1 pound pork sausage, browned, drained**
- **1/2 cup shredded cheddar cheese**
- **12 eggs, beaten**
- **1 (4 1/2 ounce) can green chilies**
- **1/2 cup self-rising flour**
- **2 cups cottage cheese**

Combine all ingredients together.
Pour into 1 1/2 quart baking dish.
Bake at 325 degrees for 45-50 minutes.

Q: Do you know why the blonde got fired from the M&M factory?
A: For throwing out the W's.

Grits Casserole

"Girls Raised In The South"

- **1 cup grits**
- **4 cups boiling water**
- **1/2 teaspoon garlic salt**
- **1/2 teaspoon pepper**
- **1 cup Velveeta cheese**
- **1 cup shredded sharp cheddar cheese**
- **1 stick margarine**
- **3 eggs, beaten**
- **1/3 cup milk**

Add grits to boiling salt and pepper water.
Cook according to package directions.
Add cheeses, margarine and **stir** until melted.
Stir in eggs and milk.
Pour into greased 9x13 dish.
Bake at 350 degrees for 1 hour.

Q: How can you tell a smart blonde from a dumb blonde?
A: The smart blondes have dark roots.

Ham and Cheese Pie

"Lazered Pie"

1/2 onion, chopped
1 cup shredded cheddar cheese
1 cup ham, chopped
1 (9 inch) pie shell, unbaked
1 (5 ounce) can evaporated milk
1 Tablespoon parsley
1/4 teaspoon dry mustard
1/8 teaspoon cayenne pepper
1 cup grits, cooked

Sprinkle first 3 ingredients in pie shell.
Mix remaining ingredients.
Pour over ham mixture.
Bake at 350 degrees for 45-50 minutes.

Q: What do you call a blonde in an institution of higher learning?
A: A visitor.

Marshmallow Roll-Ups

"Fluff Muff"

- **1 (10 count) can of biscuits**
- **3 Tablespoons margarine, softened**
- **1/4 cup cinnamon & sugar mixture**
- **30 small marshmallows**
- **1/2 cup powdered sugar**
- **2 Tablespoons milk**

Roll each biscuit out on floured surface.
Spread butter on each biscuit.
Sprinkle cinnamon & sugar on both sides.
Place 3 marshmallows in center of dough and **seal, pinching** dough together.
Place each biscuit in greased muffin tin, seamed-side down.
Bake at 350 degrees for 12 minutes.
Mix powdered sugar and milk until smooth.
Spread over cooked biscuits.

Oatmeal Banana Muffins

"Deannci Goes Bananas"

- **2 cups whole wheat flour**
- **1 cup uncooked oatmeal**
- **1 egg**
- **1 cup milk**
- **1/4 cup oil**
- **2 bananas, mashed**

Combine all ingredients together in order.
Pour in greased muffin tins.
Bake at 350 degrees for 15-20 minutes.

Peach Muffins

"Pouty Muffs"

- **1 1/2 cups self-rising flour**
- **1 cup sugar**
- **2 eggs, beaten**
- **1/2 teaspoon vanilla extract**
- **1/2 cup oil**
- **1 1/4 cups canned or fresh peaches, chopped**

Combine all ingredients together.
Spoon into greased muffin tins.
Bake at 350 degrees for 20-25 minutes.

Sausage Muffins

"Mouthful of Muff"

- **1 pound pork sausage, browned, drained**
- **1 cup all-purpose flour**
- **1 cup self-rising cornmeal**
- **1 (8 ounce) French onion dip**
- **1/2 cup milk**
- **1/8 teaspoon salt**

Mix all ingredients together.
Pour into greased muffin tins.
Bake at 375 degrees for 10-15 minutes.

Orange Breakfast Ring

"Winn Her A Ring"

- **2 (10 count) cans biscuits**
- **1/3 cup margarine, melted**
- **1 cup sugar**
- **3 ounces cream cheese, softened**
- **1/2 cup powdered sugar**
- **2 Tablespoons orange juice**

Dip biscuits in margarine, then sugar.
Line greased bundt pan with biscuits.
Bake at 350 degrees for 30 minutes
Mix together remaining ingredients.
Spread mixture over biscuits after removing from pan.

Sausage Bake

"Feel Free MacRee"

- **1 pound sausage, browned, drained**
- **8 ounces shredded cheddar cheese**
- **1 (4 1/2 ounce) can chopped mushrooms**
- **1 bell pepper, chopped**
- **1 small onion, chopped**
- **8 eggs, beaten**

Layer first 5 ingredients in 9x13 baking dish.
Pour eggs over layering.
Bake at 350 degrees for 20-25 minutes.

Sausage & Potato Casserole

"Linkin Logs"

2 packages Brown & Serve sausage links
$3^1/_2$ cups frozen hash brown potatoes
$1^1/_2$ cups shredded sharp cheddar cheese
$1^1/_4$ cups milk
7 eggs, beaten
1 ($4^1/_2$ ounce) can green chilies

Cut into slices and **brown** sausage.
Mix all ingredients together.
Pour into greased 9x13 dish.
Bake at 350 degrees for 1 hour.

Q: Why don't blondes eat pickles?
A: Because they get their heads stuck in the jar.

Baked French Toast

"Making A Toast"

- **1 loaf Texas toast, cut in diagonal 1" slices**
- **8 eggs**
- **2 cups milk**
- **1 1/2 cups half & half**
- **2 teaspoons vanilla extract**
- **1/4 teaspoon cinnamon**
- **3/4 cup margarine**
- **1 1/3 cups brown sugar**
- **3 Tablespoons corn syrup**

Arrange bread in greased 9x13 baking dish.
Beat eggs, milk, cream, vanilla, and cinnamon.
Pour over bread, **cover**, **refrigerate** over night.
Combine margarine, sugar and syrup in saucepan until bubbly.
Pour over bread and egg mixture.
Bake at 350 degrees, **uncovered** for 40 minutes.

Q: How do you confuse a blonde?
A: You don't. They're born that way.

Blonde Times Five

A blind man enters a ladies bar by mistake. He finds his way to a bar stool and orders a drink. After sitting there for awhile, he yells to the bartender "Hey, you wanna hear a dumb blonde joke?"

The bar immediately falls absolutely quiet. In a very deep, husky voice, the woman next to him says, "Before you tell that joke, sir, I think it is just fair – given that you are blind – that you should know

FIVE THINGS...

1 – The bartender is a blonde girl.
2 – The bouncer is a blonde girl.
3 – I'm a 6 feet tall, 250 lb. blonde woman with a black belt in karate.
4 – The woman sitting next to me is blonde and is a professional weightlifter.
5 – The lady to your right is a blonde and is a professional wrestler.

Now think about it seriously, Mister. Do you still wanna tell that joke?"

The blind man thinks for a second, shakes his head, and declares. "Nah ... Not if I'm gonna have to explain it five times."

Souper Nooners

(Dressings, Salads & Soups)

Souper Nooners
(Dressings, Salads & Soups)

Dressings/Sauces

Salads

Soups

Q: How do you drive a blonde crazy?
A: Put her in a round room and tell her to stand in the corner.

Balsamic Dressing

"Deannci's Favorite"

- $^2/_3$ **cup balsamic vinegar**
- 4 **Tablespoons olive oil**
- 4 **Tablespoons dry mustard**
- 2 **teaspoons basil**
- 2 **teaspoons salt**
- $^1/_2$ **teaspoon pepper**

Mix all ingredients together
Pour over favorite lettuce.

Celery Seed-Honey Dressing

"Honey Do"

- 1 **cup sugar**
- 1 **teaspoon dry mustard**
- 1 **teaspoon paprika**
- $^1/_4$ **teaspoon onion salt**
- 1 **teaspoon celery seed**
- $^1/_3$ **cup honey**
- 1 **Tablespoon lemon juice**
- 4 **Tablespoons vinegar**
- 1 **cup oil**

Mix first 8 ingredients together.
Pour oil slowly into mixture, **beating** constantly.
Serve with fruit.

Come-Back Dressing

"Come Back For Moore"

1 cup mayonnaise
1/2 cup chili sauce
1 teaspoon Worcestershire
1/2 teaspoon Tabasco
1 juice of a lemon
1 (6 ounce) can crabmeat, drained

Mix all ingredients together.
Refrigerate.
Serve on lettuce, crackers or fresh tomatoes.

Creamy Dressing

"Dreamy Creamy"

4 cups Miracle Whip dressing
1 can tomato soup
4 Tablespoons canola oil
4 Tablespoons vinegar
4 Tablespoons sugar
1/2 teaspoon salt

Combine all ingredients together.
Serve on lettuce.
Store in refrigerator.

Chunky Guacamole
"Hunky Chunky"

6 ripe avocados
1/4 cup lime juice
1/4 cup lemon juice
4 cherry tomatoes, finely chopped
6 jarred whole jalapeño peppers, finely chopped
1/4 teaspoon salt

Half avocados and **remove** pits.
Score flesh into cubes and **mix** in bowl.
Stir in remaining ingredients.

Meat Marinade
"Beat the Meat"

1 gallon apple juice
1/4 cup salt
1/4 cup pepper
1/2 cup Worchestshire
1 teaspoon hot pepper sauce
1 stick margarine, melted
1 teaspoon garlic salt
1 teaspoon garlic powder
2 teaspoons dry mustard

Mix all ingredients.
Store in refrigerator up to a month.

Poppy Seed Dressing

"Perky & Poppy"

- **3/4 cup sugar**
- **1 teaspoon dry mustard**
- **1 1/2 teaspoons salt**
- **1/3 cup vinegar**
- **1 cup oil**
- **1 Tablespoon poppy seeds**

Mix first 4 ingredients together.
Add oil slowly and **beat** 5 minutes.
Add poppy seeds and **beat** 1 minute longer.
Store in refrigerator.
Serve over any fruit.

Fresh Salsa

"Hot to Trot *Salsa*"

- **2 (28 ounce) cans crushed tomatoes**
- **5 jarred whole jalapeño peppers**
- **2 teaspoons cumin**
- **2 teaspoons salt**
- **1/2 bunch cilantro**
- **1 onion, chopped**

Place all ingredients in food processor and **blend**.
Store in refrigerator.

Spinach Salad Dressing

"Green Cream"

- **1 cup oil**
- **3/4 cup sugar**
- **1/3 cup ketchup**
- **1/2 cup red wine vinegar**
- **1 Tablespoon minced onion**
- **1 Tablespoon Worcestershire**

Mix all ingredients together.
Serve over a spinach salad.

Spaghetti Sauce

"Italian Stallion"

- **1 bell pepper, chopped**
- **1 onion, chopped**
- **1 stick margarine**
- **2 (28 ounce) cans crushed tomatoes**
- **1 (6 ounce) can tomato paste**
- **1 (10 ounce) can Rotel tomatoes**
- **1/2 cup sugar**
- **1 Tablespoon garlic salt**
- **1 Tablespoon basil**

Sauté pepper and onion in margarine.
Add all ingredients in pot.
Simmer on low for 2 hours, **add** water as needed.

24-Hour Green Vegetable Salad

"All-Nite Long"

- **1 head lettuce, chopped**
- **1 teaspoon sugar**
- **1 teaspoon salt & pepper**
- **6 hard boiled eggs, sliced**
- **1 (10 ounce) package frozen green peas, thawed**
- **1 pound bacon, cooked, drained and crumbled**
- **16 ounces shredded cheddar cheese**
- **1 cup mayonnaise**
- **1/4 cup green onions, chopped**

Place 3 cups lettuce in bottom of large glass bowl.
Sprinkle with sugar, salt and pepper.
Layer eggs over lettuce.
Layer peas, remaining lettuce, bacon and cheese.
Spread mayonnaise over top.
Chill for 24 to 48 hours.
Garnish with green onions.

Q: Why don't blondes make kool-aid?
A: Can't fit 8 cups of water in the little packages.

Black Bean Salad

"Magical Beans"

2 (15 ounce) cans black beans, drained
2 cups white rice, cooked
1 1/2 Tablespoons olive oil
2 Tablespoons balsamic vinegar
1 green bell pepper, chopped
1 red bell pepper, chopped
1/2 cup green onion, chopped
1/4 cup cilantro, chopped
1/8 teaspoon salt

Mix all ingredients together.
Refrigerate.

Final Exam

The blonde reported for her university final examination that consists of yes/no type questions. She takes her seat in the examination hall, stares at the question on the paper for five minutes and then in a fit of inspiration, takes out her purse, removes a coin and starts tossing the coin, marking the answer sheet: Yes, for Heads, and No, for Tails. Within half an hour she is all done, whereas the rest of the class is still sweating it out. During the last few minutes she is seen desperately throwing the coin, muttering and sweating. The moderator, alarmed, approaches her and asks what is going on. "I finished the exam in half an hour, but now I'm rechecking my answers."

Cheesy Italian Salad

"Blue Balls"

- **3 zucchini, finely chopped**
- **4 green onions, sliced**
- **8 ounces fresh sliced mushrooms**
- **1 hard boiled egg, finely chopped**
- **1 clove garlic, crushed**
- **1 (12 ounce) package crumbled blue cheese**
- **1 tomato, chopped**
- **1/2 cup Italian dressing**
- **1 small head lettuce**

Combine first 8 ingredients together.
Cover and **refrigerate** for 2 hours.
Cut lettuce into big wedges.
Pour mixture on top of lettuce.

Q: How can you tell when a fax had been sent from a blonde?
A: There is a stamp on it.

Chicken & Pasta Salad

"Chick-A-P"

6 grilled chicken breasts, chopped
1 (16 ounce) bag spiral pasta, cooked
1 red bell pepper, chopped
1 green bell pepper, chopped
1 squash, julienne sliced
1 zucchini, julienne sliced
8 ounces shredded cheddar cheese

Dressing:
1 cup ranch dressing
1 (16 ounce) jar medium salsa

Mix all ingredients together.
Toss with dressing until pasta is all coated.

Cranberry Salad

"Granny Cranny"

2 (3 ounce) boxes raspberry jello
1 cup hot water
1 (8 ounce) can crushed pineapple
1 (16 ounce) can whole cranberry sauce
1/2 cup pecans
8 ounces Cool Whip
2 bananas, mashed

Dissolve jello in hot water.
Mix all ingredients together in order.
Refrigerate.
Cut into squares.

Fruit Salad

"My C Cup Runneth Over"

1 cup seedless grapes
1/2 cup mandarin oranges
1/2 cup cantaloupe, chopped
1/2 cup banana, sliced
1/2 cup pineapple chunks
1/4 cup orange juice concentrate, thawed
1 teaspoon lime juice
2 teaspoon minced mint
1/4 teaspoon grated lime zest

Combine all ingredients together in a large bowl.
Toss gently.

Grape Salad

"Sugar Coated"

3 pounds seedless grapes, stems removed
1 (8 ounce) cream cheese, softened
1/2 cup powdered sugar
1/2 teaspoon vanilla extract
1/2 teaspoon almond extract
1 (8 ounce) sour cream
1/2 cup brown sugar
1/2 stick margarine, melted
1 cup pecans, chopped

Place grapes in 9x13 dish.
Cream next 4 ingredients together.
Spread over grapes.
Mix next 2 ingredients, **pour** over cream cheese mixture.
Sprinkle with pecans.

Mexican Chef Salad

"Fiesta Time"

1 pound ground beef, cooked, drained
1 onion, chopped
1 tomato, chopped
1 head lettuce, shredded
1 ripe avocado, peeled, pitted, cubed
16 ounces shredded cheddar cheese
1 (16 ounce) can kidney beans, drained
1 (16 ounce) bottle Thousand Island dressing
1 (15 ounce) bag tortilla chips

Mix first 8 ingredients together.
Serve over chips.

Orange Salad

"Orange U Glad To See Me"

2 (3 ounce) boxes orange jello
1 cup boiling water
1 (15 ounce) can crushed pineapple
1 (11 ounce) can mandarin oranges
1 (12 ounce) cottage cheese
1 (8 ounce) Cool Whip

Mix all ingredients together.
Refrigerate.

Oriental Salad

"Flamin Ramen

1	**(1 pound) bag cole slaw**
1/4	**cup green onions, chopped**
1	**(3 3/4 ounce) package sunflower kernels**
1	**(2.0 ounce) package slivered almonds**
1/2	**teaspoon pepper**
2	**packages Ramen Oriental instant soup**

Dressing: Mix together in shaker.

3/4	**cup oil**
1/4	**cup sugar**
1/2	**cup vinegar**
1/2	**teaspoon of salt**
1/2	**teaspoon of pepper**
2	**packages seasoning from noodles**

Combine first 5 ingredients and **toss**.
Mix all dressings ingredients together.
Break noodles into small pieces.
Sprinkle noodles just prior to serving.
Add dressing, **toss**.

Q: Why don't blondes make good pharmacists?
A: They can't get the bottle into the typewriter.

Pasta Artichoke Salad

"Chokin"

- **1** **(16 ounce) package angel hair pasta, cooked, drained**
- **1** **(4 ounce) jar sliced pimientos**
- **1** **(4 1/4 ounce) can chopped black olives**
- **1** **bell pepper, chopped**
- **1/2** **cup olive oil**
- **3** **Tablespoons lemon juice**
- **3** **Tablespoons mayonnaise**
- **3** **Tablespoons Cavendars Greek seasoning**
- **1** **(14 ounce) can artichoke hearts, chopped**

Mix all ingredients together and **refrigerate**.

Pasta Prima Vera Salad

"Ice Princess"

- **1** **(12 ounce) package rotini pasta, cooked, drained**
- **1** **cup cherry tomatoes, quartered**
- **2** **cups broccoli florets**
- **1** **cup carrots, sliced**
- **1/4** **cup red onion, chopped**
- **1** **(8 ounce) bottle Peppercorn Ranch Dressing**

Mix all ingredients together and **refrigerate**.

Potato Salad

"Stud Potato"

- **6 medium red potatoes**
- **4 boiled eggs**
- **1/4 cup Italian dressing**
- **1/4 cup chopped sweet pickles**
- **1/4 cup onion, chopped**
- **1/4 cup mayonnaise**

Peel and **chop** potatoes.
Boil potatoes until tender.
Boil eggs and **chop**.
Toss all ingredients together.

Kidnapped Blonde

There was a blonde woman who was having financial troubles so she decided to kidnap a child and demand a ransom. She went to a local park, grabbed a little boy, took him behind a tree and wrote this note: I have kidnapped your child. Leave $10,000 in a brown bag behind the big oak tree. Just as she had instructed, inside the bag was the following note..... Here is your money. I cannot believe that one blonde would do this to another!

Pretzel Salad

"Twisted"

Crust:

2 cups pretzels, crushed
1/4 cup sugar
1 1/2 sticks margarine, melted

Layer 1:

1 (8 ounce) cream cheese, softened
1 cup sugar
1 (8 ounce) Cool Whip

Layer 2:

2 cups pineapple juice
2 (3 ounce) boxes strawberry jello
2 (10 ounce) packages frozen strawberries

Mix crust ingredients and **spread** in greased 9x13 pan.
Bake at 350 degrees for 10 minutes.
Mix layer 1 ingredients together.
Spread over cooled crust.
Boil the juice for layer 2.
Dissolve jello in juice.
Add the strawberries.
Set in refrigerator for about 5-10 minutes.
Spread this over layer 1.
Refrigerate.

Q: How do you get a blonde's eyes to sparkle?
A: Shine a light in her ear.

Rice Salad

"Brainy Grainy"

- 1 cup long grain rice
- 1 avocado, chopped
- 1 (14 ounce) can artichoke hearts, chopped
- 1 ($4^{1}/_{4}$ ounce) can chopped black olives
- $^{1}/_{2}$ teaspoon salt
- 1 cup Italian dressing

Cook rice according to directions.
Combine next 5 ingredients.
Mix all ingredients together.

Waldorf Rice Salad

"Jazza Barazza"

- 1 (11 ounce) can mandarin oranges, drained
- 1 apple, unpeeled, chopped
- 1 pear, unpeeled, chopped
- 2 cups rice, cooked
- $^{1}/_{2}$ cup celery, chopped
- $^{1}/_{3}$ cup raisins
- $^{1}/_{2}$ cup mayonnaise
- $^{1}/_{4}$ cup sour cream
- $^{1}/_{2}$ cup walnuts, chopped, toasted

Combine first 6 ingredients together.
Stir in mayonnaise and sour cream.
Sprinkle with walnuts just before serving.

Romaine Mandarin Orange Salad

"Roaming Eyes"

- **1 (16 ounce) bag romaine lettuce**
- **1 (11 ounce) can mandarin oranges, drained**
- **2/3 cup olive oil**
- **1/2 cup balsamic vinegar**
- **1 teaspoon prepared mustard**
- **1 Tablespoon poppy seeds**

Combine lettuce, oranges in salad bowl.
Mix rest of ingredients together.
Pour on lettuce when ready to serve.

Rotel Pasta Salad

"Rockin Rotel"

- **1 (16 ounce) package favorite pasta**
- **1 package dry Italian salad mix**
- **1 (10 ounce) can Rotel tomatoes**
- **1/2 cup balsamic vinegar**
- **1 cup Italian dressing**
- **1 (4 1/4 ounce) can chopped black olives**

Cook pasta according to directions.
Combine all ingredients together.

Summer Egg Salad

"She's All Cracked Up"

- **1 (3 ounce) cream cheese, softened**
- **1/4 cup mayonnaise**
- **1/4 teaspoon dill weed**
- **1/4 teaspoon salt**
- **6 hard boiled eggs, chopped**
- **1/2 cup green olives, chopped**
- **1/2 cup celery, chopped**
- **2 Tablespoons onion, chopped**
- **1 Tablespoon sliced pimiento**

Blend first 4 ingredients together.
Add next 5 ingredients.
Keep refrigerated until ready to serve.

Vegetable Pasta Salad

"Scattered Blondes"

- **1 (12 ounce) package pasta**
- **1/2 cup green olives, chopped**
- **1 (4 1/4 ounce) can chopped black olives**
- **1 (2 ounce) jar sliced pimientos**
- **1 bell pepper, chopped**
- **3 roma tomatoes, chopped**
- **1 Tablespoon capers**
- **1/2 cup balsamic vinegar**
- **1/2 cup parmesan cheese**

Cook pasta according to directions.
Mix all ingredients together.

Cream of Broccoli Soup

"Butchy Green Cream"

- **2 sticks margarine**
- **1 cup flour**
- **$^1/_2$ teaspoon pepper**
- **1 onion, chopped**
- **1 celery stalk, chopped**
- **1 (16 ounce) bag frozen chopped broccoli**
- **3 (14$^1/_2$ ounce) cans chicken broth**
- **2 pounds Velveeta cheese, cubed**
- **$^1/_2$ pint whipping cream**

Melt butter and gradually **add** next 2 ingredients, **stirring** constantly.
Stir in next 4 ingredients.
Simmer for 30 minutes.
Reduce heat and add cheese.
Cook until cheese melts.
Stir in whipping cream and **cook** until heated.

Q: Why did the blonde have tire tread marks on her back?
A: From crawling across the street when the sign said, "Don't Walk."

Chicken Noodle Soup

"Naughty Nurse Brew

- **3 (14½ ounce) cans chicken broth**
- **½ cup onion, chopped**
- **½ cup celery, chopped**
- **1 cup carrots, chopped**
- **3 chicken breasts, cooked, diced**
- **1 cup egg noodles, cooked**

Mix first 4 ingredients together and **bring** to a boil. **Lower** heat to simmer and **cook** for 20 minutes. **Add** chicken and **cook** for 10 more minutes. **Add** cooked noodles and **heat** through.

Chicken Tortilla Soup

"Tingling All Over"

- **3 boneless, skinless chicken breasts**
- **1 (10 ounce) can diced Rotel tomatoes**
- **1 (11 ounce) can Mexicorn**
- **1 (14½ ounce) can chicken broth**
- **1 (4½ ounce) can green chilies**
- **1 package dry taco seasoning mix**
- **8-10 flour tortillas, cut in strips**
- **4 cups water**
- **8 ounces shredded mozzarella cheese**

Mix first 8 ingredients together and **bring** to a boil. **Lower** heat to a simmer and **cook** for 20 minutes. **Add** cheese and **heat** through.

Easy Chili

"She's Easy"

- **1 pound ground chuck**
- **1/2 onion, chopped**
- **2 (16 ounce) cans red kidney beans, drained**
- **2 (14 1/2 ounce) cans diced tomatoes**
- **3 Tablespoons chili powder**
- **salt and pepper to taste**

Brown meat and onions, **draining** well.
Add remaining ingredients.
Bring to boil. **Add** water if needed.
Simmer at least 2 hours.

White Chili

"Bleached Blonde"

- **4 chicken breasts, cooked, diced**
- **3 (16 ounce) cans northern beans**
- **3 (14.5 ounce) cans chicken broth**
- **1 (4.5 ounce) can chopped green chilies**
- **8 ounces shredded Monterey Jack cheese**
- **2 Tablespoons oregano**
- **2 teaspoons cumin**
- **1 (12 ounce) can shoe peg corn**
- **1/2 teaspoon cayenne pepper**

Add all ingredients together.
Simmer for 1 hour.

Turkey Corn Crowder

"Tantalizing Turkey"

5 cups water
3 celery stalks, chopped
3 cups turkey, cooked
4 Tablespoons margarine
1 (15 ounce) can cream-style corn
1 (15 1/4 ounce) can whole corn, drained
2 (14 1/2 ounce) cans chicken broth
1 teaspoon salt
3 potatoes, peeled, diced

Combine first 8 ingredients together in a large pot.
Cook on low for 1 hour.
Add potatoes and **cook** until potatoes are tender.

Oyster Stew

"Get Some"

1/2 onion, chopped
4 celery stalks, chopped
1 bell pepper, chopped
1 stick margarine
1 (14 ounce) can artichoke hearts, chopped
2 (12 ounce) cans oysters, with juice
1/2 teaspoon basil
1/2 teaspoon Italian seasoning
1/2 teaspoon salt

Combine all ingredients together.
Cook on medium for 1 hour.

Picante Soup

"Call Me Hottie"

- **1 pound ground beef**
- **1 onion, chopped**
- **2 teaspoons chili powder**
- **1 teaspoon cumin**
- **2 (14¾ ounce) cans beef broth**
- **1½ cups picante sauce**
- **1 (15 ounce) can diced tomatoes**
- **1 (8 ounce) package rotini pasta, uncooked**
- **4 ounces shredded cheddar cheese**

Brown beef and onion and **drain**.
Sprinkle chili powder and cumin over beef and **blend**.
Add next 4 ingredients.
Bring to a boil and **reduce** heat.
Cover and **simmer** for 15-20 minutes.
Serve with cheese on top.

Q: Why do blondes have T.G.I.F. printed on their shoes?
A: Stands for Toes Go In First.

Pizza Soup

"Bartz Brew"

1 pound ground beef
1 small onion, chopped
1 (7 ounce) can mushrooms, stems & pieces
1 bell pepper, cut in strips
1 (14$^3/_4$ ounce) can beef broth
1 teaspoon basil
4 ounces shredded mozzarella cheese

Brown first 4 ingredients and **drain**.
Stir all ingredients together, except cheese
Cook for 30 minutes on low.
Sprinkle cheese on top when **ready** to serve.

Q: What are the worst six years in a blonde's life?
A: Third Grade.

Potato Soup

"Spud Stud"

- **3 celery stalks, chopped**
- **1 stick margarine**
- **1/2 gallon milk**
- **4 Tablespoons cornstarch**
- **1/4 cup water**
- **2 (14 1/2 ounce) cans chicken broth**
- **1 teaspoon salt**
- **1 teaspoon pepper**
- **6 potatoes cooked, peeled, diced**

Sauté celery in margarine in large pot.
Add milk to celery mixture.
Bring mixture to a boil.
Dissolve cornstarch in water.
Combine all ingredients except potatoes.
Simmer for 30 minutes, **stirring** as it thickens.
Add potatoes and **simmer** another 15 minutes.

Q: How does a blonde know if she's on her way home or on her way to work?
A: She opens her lunch box to see if there is anything in it.

Seafood Chowder

"Chow Down"

- 2 cans cream of celery soup
- 2 soup cans milk
- 1 stick margarine
- 1/4 teaspoon ground bay leaves
- 1/4 teaspoon cayenne pepper
- 1/4 teaspoon garlic salt
- 1/2 teaspoon thyme
- 1 (6 ounce) can crabmeat, drained
- 1 (4 1/2 ounce) can shrimp, drained

Combine all ingredients together.
Simmer on low for 1 hour.

Taco Soup

"Macho Man"

- 2 pounds ground meat, cooked, drained
- 2 (10 ounce) cans chopped Rotel tomatoes
- 2 packages taco seasoning mix
- 2 (12 ounce) cans shoe peg corn
- 2 packages dry Ranch dressing mix
- 1 (16 ounce) can kidney beans, drained
- 1 (15 ounce) can black beans, drained
- 1 (16 ounce) can navy beans, drained
- 2 (14 1/2 ounce) cans diced tomatoes

Mix all ingredients together.
Cook on medium for 1 hour.
Add 1-2 cups of water as needed.

Cheesy Vegetable Chowder

"Easy Cheesy"

- **1/2 onion, chopped**
- **1 teaspoon garlic salt and celery salt**
- **4 carrots, sliced**
- **3 potatoes, peeled, cubed**
- **2 (14 1/2 ounce) cans chicken broth**
- **2 cups warmed milk**
- **1 (15 1/4 ounce) can whole corn, drained**
- **1/4 cup margarine & flour**
- **8 ounces Velveeta cheese**

Combine first 5 ingredients in large pot.
Bring to a boil.
Reduce heat and **simmer** 20 minutes until potatoes are tender.
Stir in corn and **remove** from heat.
Melt margarine in separate saucepan. **Stir** in flour until smooth.
Add warmed milk slowly until thick.
Add cheese until melted, **stirring** constantly.
Gradually stir cheese sauce into vegetables.
Warm slowly.

Q: How many blondes does it take to change a tire?
A: 5—2 to get sodas, 2 to cry and 1 to call daddy.

Wild Rice Soup

"Wild Thang"

- **3 chicken breasts, cooked, diced.**
- **2 (14 1/2 ounce) cans chicken broth**
- **2 boxes Uncle Ben's Wild Rice, cooked**
- **1 1/2 cups long grain white rice, cooked**
- **1 (8 ounce) sour cream**
- **1 pound Velveeta cheese, cubed**

Mix first 5 ingredients together.
Simmer on low for 30 minues.
Add cheese until melts.

Won Ton Soup

"Wrap Her Up"

- **2 (14 1/2 ounce) cans chicken broth**
- **1 (14 3/4 ounce) can beef broth**
- **2 chicken bouillon cubes**
- **3 chicken breasts, cooked, chopped**
- **1 (16 ounce) egg roll wrappers, (speciality produce section)**
- **1/2 cup green onions, chopped**

Mix first 3 ingredients together.
Cook on medium high until boiling.
Cut wrappers into quarters, **twist** 2 pieces together.
Drop wrappers in boiling broth.
Add last 2 ingredients.
Simmer on low for 30 minutes.

Cream of the Crop

(Vegetables & More)

Cream of the Crop
(Vegetables & More)

Vegetables

Q: How do you give a blonde a brain transplant?
A: Blow in her ear.

Artichoke Casserole

"My Heart Is Chokin' "

- **2 (14 ounce) cans artichoke hearts, drained**
- **1/2 cup olive oil**
- **1 cup water**
- **1 cup Italian breadcrumbs**
- **1/4 cup minced garlic**
- **3 ounces romano cheese**

Cut artichokes into quarters.
Add oil and water to artichokes and **mix**.
Add remaining ingredients.
Put in 9x13 baking dish.
Bake at 400 degrees **covered** for 30 minutes.

Artichoke Mushroom Bake

"Road To My Heart"

- **2 (14 ounce) cans artichoke hearts, drained**
- **1 stick margarine**
- **8 ounces fresh mushrooms, sliced**
- **1 (8 ounce) sour cream**
- **1 teaspoon Worcestershire**
- **1/4 cup breadcrumbs**

Put artichoke hearts in 9x9 baking dish.
Sauté rest of ingredients in margarine for 10 minutes.
Pour over artichoke hearts.
Bake at 350 degrees for 30-45 minutes.

Asparagus Casserole

"Aspiring for Us"

- **1 sleeve saltine crackers, crushed**
- **1 (12 ounce) can asparagus**
- **1 can cream of mushroom soup**
- **1/2 stick margarine**
- **2 eggs, boiled, chopped**
- **8 ounces shredded cheddar cheese**

Sprinkle crackers in 9x13 baking dish.
Place asparagus over crackers.
Heat soup and margarine for 5 minutes.
Add eggs and cheese to soup mixture.
Pour over asparagus.
Bake at 350 degrees for 20-30 minutes.

Baked Beans

"Blonde Body Guards"

- **1 (10 ounce) can Kelly's Pork with Barbecue Sauce**
- **1/3 cup vinegar**
- **1/2 onion, chopped**
- **2 Tablespoons steak sauce**
- **2 teaspoons mustard**
- **2 (16 ounce) cans pork & beans**
- **1/2 cup brown sugar**
- **1/2 Tablespoon garlic powder**
- **1 Tablespoon ketchup**

Mix all ingredients together.
Bake at 350 degrees for 1 hour.

Beets

"Beet Me"

- **2 (15 ounce) cans beets**
- **1 Tablespoon cornstarch**
- **1/2 cup sugar**
- **1/4 cup water**
- **1/2 cup white vinegar**
- **1/2 teaspoon salt**

Cook beets in a little water for 15 minutes.
Mix all other ingredients in separate pan.
Cook slowly until mixture is clear.
Stir while cooking.
Pour over beets.
Let stand for 15 minutes before serving.

In a Vacuum

A blonde was playing Trivial Pursuit one night. It was her turn. She rolled the dice and she landed on Science & Nature. Her question was, If you are in a vacuum and someone calls your name, can you hear it? She thought for a time and then asked, "Is it on or off?"

Stuffed Bell Peppers

"Stuff Her Bell"

1 pound ground beef
$^{1}/_{2}$ onion, chopped
1 Tablespoon oil
1 (14$^{1}/_{2}$ ounce) can stewed tomatoes
$^{3}/_{4}$ cup rice, cooked
2 Tablespoons Worcestershire
6 bell peppers
8 ounces shredded cheddar cheese
salt to taste

Brown meat and onion in oil, **drain**.
Add next 4 ingredients to meat mixture.
Cut top off bell peppers and **clean** seeds out.
Cook peppers in salted water until boiling, then **drain**.
Stuff meat mixture into bell peppers.
Bake at 350 degrees, covered for 40 minutes.
Sprinkle cheese on peppers and **bake** until melted.

Q: What does a blonde say when you blow in her ear?
A: Thanks for the refill.

Broccoli Casserole

"Busty & Bushy"

- **1 stick margarine, softened**
- **1/2 onion, chopped**
- **1 can cream of mushroom soup**
- **2 (10 ounce) packages frozen chopped broccoli**
- **1 cup rice, cooked**
- **1 (15 ounce) jar Cheez Whiz**

Mix all ingredients together.
Bake covered at 350 degrees for 1 hour.

Cabbage Au Gratin

"Get Lucky"

- **1 head of cabbage, chopped, boiled, drained**
- **2 Tablespoons margarine**
- **2 Tablespoons flour**
- **1 cup milk**
- **1/4 cup breadcrumbs**
- **8 ounces shredded cheddar cheese**

Put cabbage in 9x13 baking dish.
Combine next 3 ingredients in saucepan until thick.
Pour mixture over cabbage.
Top with breadcrumbs and cheese.
Bake at 350 degrees for 30-45 minutes.

Carrots
"Caressing"

1	**pound carrots, sliced**
1 1/4	**cups water**
1/3	**cup golden raisins**
1/2	**cup honey**
2	**Tablespoons butter**
1	**teaspoon brown sugar**

Cook carrots in water.
Cover and **simmer** for 20 minutes.
Add remaining ingredients.
Cook uncovered for 10 more minutes.

Corn Bake
"Blondes Being Corny"

1	**(8 1/2 ounce) box Jiffy cornbread mix**
1	**(15 ounce) can cream-style corn**
1	**(15 1/4 ounce) can whole corn, undrained**
1	**(8 ounce) sour cream**
1	**egg**
1	**stick margarine, softened**

Mix all ingredients together.
Pour into greased 2 quart dish.
Bake at 350 degrees for 45-55 minutes.

Corn Casserole
"Ritzy Corn"

4 Tablespoons flour
3 Tablespoons margarine, softened
1 cup milk
1 can cream of chicken soup
3 (15 1/4 ounce) cans whole corn, drained
1/2 teaspoon salt
1/2 teaspoon pepper
1 stick margarine, melted
36 Ritz crackers, crushed

Mix first 3 ingredients together.
Add next 4 ingredients.
Cook until thickened.
Pour into greased 2 quart casserole dish.
Mix the stick of margarine and crackers.
Spread on top of mixture.
Bake at 350 degrees for 20-30 minutes.

Q: How do you confuse a blonde?
A: Put three shovels against the wall and tell her .... to take her "PICK."

Eggplant Casserole

"It's Fertile"

1 eggplant, peeled, sliced
1 egg, beaten
1 bell pepper, chopped
1 onion, chopped
16 ounces shredded cheddar cheese
1 can cream of mushroom soup
$^{1}/_{2}$ cup cracker crumbs
2 Tablespoons oil, divided
salt and pepper to taste

Cook eggplant until tender.
Drain and **mash** eggplant and **add** egg.
Sauté bell pepper and onion in 1 tablespoon oil.
Add eggplant with 1 cup cheese.
Add cracker crumbs that have been soaked in just enough milk to wet thoroughly.
Add soup and 1 tablespoon oil.
Put in 2 quart casserole dish.
Bake at 350 degrees for 30 minutes.
Add rest of cheese and **cook** 20 minutes more.

Q: What do you do when a blonde throws a grenade at you?
A: Pull the pin and throw it back.

Eggplant Parmesan

"Extra Fertile"

- **1 eggplant**
- **3 eggs, beaten**
- **1/2 cup Italian breadcrumbs**
- **1/4 cup parmesan cheese**
- **1/8 teaspoon garlic salt**
- **1/4 cup olive oil**
- **8 ounces ricotta cheese**
- **1 (26 ounce) jar spaghetti sauce**
- **8 ounces shredded mozzarella cheese**

Slice eggplant about 1/2 inch thick.
Dip eggplant in 2 beaten eggs.
Combine next 3 ingredients together.
Dip eggplant in breadcrumb mixture.
Fry in oil on low until brown on both sides.
Mix ricotta cheese and 3rd egg together.
Place 1/2 fried eggplant in 9x13 baking dish.
Put ricotta cheese mixture on each eggplant.
Put spaghetti sauce over cheese mixture.
Sprinkle with mozzarella cheese.
Repeat layers.
Bake at 350 degrees for 45-55 minutes.

Q: Why did the blonde climb over the glass wall?
A: To see what was on the other side.

English Pea Casserole

"Push Him Up"

2 (16 ounce) cans LeSuer peas
1/2 cup onion, chopped
1 can cream of mushroom soup
1 can cream of chicken soup
8 ounces shredded cheddar cheese
1 cup Ritz crackers, crushed

Drain peas and put in 9x13 dish.
Sprinkle onions over peas.
Combine soups together and **pour** over peas.
Cover with cheese and cracker crumbs.
Bake at 350 degrees for 20 minutes.

Green Beans

"Green Beans Gone Wild"

1 (14 1/2 ounce) can cut green beans
2 Tablespoons vinegar
2 Tablespoons sugar
1 Tablespoon margarine
1 teaspoon Worcestershire
1 teaspoon pepper

Mix all ingredients in a saucepan.
Cook down until juice is almost gone.
Pour enough water to cover beans.
Cook down again.

Macaroni & Cheese Casserole

"Pasty & Stringy"

1 (8 ounce) package elbow macaroni
1/4 cup onion, finely chopped
1/4 cup bell pepper, finely chopped
1 Tablespoon oil
1 can cream of mushroom soup
1 cup mayonnaise
8 ounces shredded sharp cheddar cheese

Cook macaroni according to directions and **drain**.
Sauté pepper and onion in oil.
Add next 2 ingredients to pepper and onions.
Alternate layers of macaroni, cheese and soup mixture in 2 quart casserole dish.
Bake at 350 degrees until bubbly.

Black-Eyed Peas & Tomatoes

"Let's Have A Face-Lift"

1 pound sausage
1 onion, chopped
1 teaspoon minced garlic
2 (10 ounce) bags frozen black-eyed peas
1 (14 1/2 ounce) can diced tomatoes
1/4 cup water
1 teaspoon chili powder
1/4 teaspoon salt
1/4 teaspoon pepper

Brown first 3 ingredients and **drain**.
Combine all ingredients in saucepan.
Simmer for 1 hour.

Cajun Potatoes

"Ragin' Cajun Stud"

6 potatoes, unpeeled
1 stick margarine, melted
1 envelope dry onion soup mix
3/4 cup water
1 Tablespoon Tony Chacheres
12 ounces shredded sharp cheddar cheese

Slice potatoes and **place** in 9x13 dish.
Mix next 4 ingredients in bowl.
Pour over potatoes.
Bake on 350 degrees, covered, for 1 hour.
Uncover, **add** cheese and **heat** to melt cheese.

Crock Pot Potatoes

"He's A Crock"

1 (3 ounce) cream cheese, softened
1/2 cup sour cream
1/2 stick margarine, softened
1 teaspoon parsley
8 potatoes, boiled, mashed
1 envelope dry Ranch dressing mix

Mix ingredients in order listed.
Put in crock pot.
Cook on low for 3 to 4 hours.

Hash Brown Potatoes

"Bodacious Ta Ta's"

1 (32 ounce) bag frozen cubed hash browns
8 ounces shredded cheddar cheese
1 can cream of chicken soup
1/2 cup sour cream
1/2 cup French onion dip
1 teaspoon salt

Mix all ingredients together.
Bake in 9x13 dish at 350 degrees for 1 hour.

Sweet Potato Casserole

"Sweet Stud"

2 large sweet potatoes, cooked, mashed
1 cup sugar
1/2 teaspoon salt
3 eggs, beaten
1/2 cup milk
1 teaspoon vanilla extract
1 cup brown sugar
1/2 cup pecans, chopped
4 Tablespoons margarine

Mix first 6 ingredients together.
Spread evenly in 9x13 dish.
Mix the next 3 ingredients and **sprinkle** evenly over casserole.
Bake at 300 degrees for 30 minutes.

Dirty Rice

"Let's Get Down & Dirty"

- 2 Tablespoons margarine
- 2 Tablespoons minced onion
- 1 cup uncooked rice
- 1 can beef consommé soup
- 1 can onion soup
- 1 (7 ounce) mushroom stems & pieces

Melt margarine and onion in skillet until light brown.
Add rice and **cook** over medium heat until brown.
Stir to prevent burning.
Add next 3 ingredients.
Put in 9x13 dish.
Cover and **bake** at 350 degrees for 1 hour.

Spinach Casserole

"I Need Mo Money"

- 2 (10 ounce) packages frozen chopped spinach, cooked, drained
- 2 eggs, beaten
- 1 (8 ounce) sour cream
- 1/3 cup parmesan cheese
- 8 ounces jalapeño cheese
- salt & pepper to taste

Mix all ingredients together.
Put in 9x13 dish.
Bake at 300 degrees for 30 to 40 minutes.

Squash Casserole

"Squeezy Blonde"

- **4 yellow squash, sliced**
- **1 can cream of chicken soup**
- **1 (8 ounce) sour cream**
- **2 carrots, chopped**
- **2 sticks margarine, softened**
- **1 (6 ounce) box Pepperidge Farm Cornbread Stuffing**

Cook squash until tender and **mash**.
Combine with next 3 ingredients.
Melt margarine and **combine** with stuffing.
Layer 1/2 squash mixture, 1/2 stuffing in 2 quart casserole dish.
Repeat layers.
Bake at 400 degrees for 20 minutes.

Speeding Ticket

A police officer stops a blonde for speeding and asks her very nicely if he could see her license. She replied in a huff, "I wish you guys would get your act together. Just yesterday you took away my license and then today you expect me to show it to you!"

Squash Medley

"Blonde Medley"

- **1/4 cup onion, chopped**
- **2 Tablespoons margarine**
- **1 (15 1/4 ounce) can whole corn**
- **3 tomatoes, peeled, chopped**
- **4 yellow squash, sliced**
- **1 teaspoon salt**
- **3/4 teaspoon dried whole oregano**
- **1/2 teaspoon sugar**
- **1/4 teaspoon pepper**

Sauté onion in margarine.
Add remaining ingredients in large saucepan.
Cover and **cook** for 20-30 minutes.

Q: Why is the blonde's brain the size of a pea in the morning?
A: It swells at night.

Tomato Casserole

"To Mate"

- **1 onion, diced**
- **1 bell pepper, diced**
- **2 Tablespoons olive oil**
- **2 (14 1/2 ounce) cans diced tomatoes**
- **2 teaspoons creole seasoning**
- **4 Tablespoons brown sugar**
- **4 Tablespoons Worcestershire**
- **1 cup breadcrumbs**
- **dash of hot sauce**

Sauté first 2 ingredients in olive oil until tender.
Mix all ingredients together.
Put in 9x13 baking dish.
Bake at 350 degrees for 25-30 minutes.

Tomato Pie

"To Mate Tonight"

- **1 (9 inch) pie shell**
- **2 fresh tomatoes, sliced**
- **3/4 bunch green onions, chopped**
- **1 Tablespoon fresh basil**
- **1 cup mayonnaise**
- **8 ounces shredded Monterey Jack cheese**

Cook pie shells for 10 minutes on 350 degrees
Line bottom of pie shells with tomatoes.
Add green onions, basil and **salt** and **pepper** to taste.
Mix mayonnaise with cheese.
Spread over pie, **sealing** to edges.
Bake at 400 degrees for 20 minutes.

Veg-All Casserole

"Veg-Out

- **2 (15 ounce) cans Veg-All, drained**
- **1 cup mayonnaise**
- **1 cup chopped celery**
- **1 cup chopped onion**
- **1 cup shredded cheddar cheese**
- **1 1/2 cups Ritz crackers, crushed**

Combine first 5 ingredients .
Put in 2 quart casserole dish.
Melt 4 Tablespoons of butter and **mix** with Ritz crackers.
Sprinkle on top of mixture.
Bake for 20 minutes at 350.

Q: Why did the blonde stay up all night to see where the sun went?
A: It finally dawned on her.

Vidalia Onion Casserole

"Sweet Kisses"

4 Vidalia onions, sliced in rings
1 stick margarine, divided
1 1/2 packs Ritz crackers, crushed
8 ounces shredded sharp cheddar cheese
3 large eggs, beaten
1 cup milk

Sauté onion rings in 1/4 cup margarine.
Combine remaining margarine with crackers (**saving** some crackers for topping).
Layer crumbs into bottom of greased 9x13 dish.
Spread onions over crumbs, **sprinkle** with cheese.
Combine eggs and milk.
Pour over onions & cheese.
Sprinkle with crumbs.
Bake at 350 degrees for 35 to 40 minutes.

Q: Why do blondes wear ear muffs?
A: To avoid the draft.

Zucchini Oriental

"Chelly Does China"

- **1/3 cup olive oil**
- **8 ounces fresh sliced mushrooms**
- **1 small purple onion, thinly sliced**
- **1 bunch green onions, chopped**
- **1 medium zucchini, cut in 3 inch strips**
- **1/2 teaspoon sugar**
- **1/2 teaspoon black pepper**
- **2 Tablespoons soy sauce**
- **1 cup cooked rice**

Pour olive oil into preheated wok or large skillet.
Add next 4 ingredients.
Stir fry for 4 to 5 minutes.
Combine next 3 ingredients together.
Pour over vegetable mixture and **simmer** 3 minutes.
Serve over rice.

Q: What is the blonde doing when she holds her hands over her ears?
A: Trying to hold on to a thought.

Enter Courses

(Beef, Chicken, Pork & Seafood)

Enter Courses
Beef, Chicken, Pork & Seafood

Beef

Chicken

Pork

Seafood

Beef Eggplant
"Purple Meat"

- **2 pounds ground beef**
- **1 teaspoon Worcestershire**
- **1 eggplant, peeled, cubed**
- **1/4 cup milk**
- **2 eggs**
- **1 (15 ounce) can cream-style corn**
- **8 ounces shredded cheddar cheese**
- **1/2 cup breadcrumbs**
- **salt & pepper to taste**

Brown beef and **drain**.
Add next 7 ingredients to beef.
Pour into 9 x13 greased baking dish.
Top with breadcrumbs.
Bake at 350 degrees **uncovered** for 50-60 minutes.

Q: What is it called when a blonde blows in another blonde's ear?
A: Data transfer.

Beef Stroganoff

"Meat with a Limp"

$1^1/_2$ pounds ground chuck
$^1/_4$ cup green onion, chopped
1 Tablespoon minced garlic
1 (7 ounce) can mushroom stems & pieces
$^1/_2$ cup cooking sherry
3 Tablespoons lemon juice
1 can beef consommé soup
1 (16 ounce) package egg noodles
1 (8 ounce) sour cream

Cook beef and **drain**.
Add next 6 ingredients to beef and **sauté**.
Simmer for 15 minutes.
Cook noodles according to package and **drain**.
Add noodles and sour cream to meat mixture.
Mix all ingredients together, thoroughly.

Q: Why did the blonde put her finger over the nail when she was hammering?
A: The noise gave her a headache.

Chinese Hamburger

"Chinaburger"

1 pound ground beef
1 onion, chopped
1 can cream of mushroom soup
1 can cream of chicken soup
1/4 cup soy sauce
1/2 cup Minute Rice, uncooked
3 celery stalks, chopped
1 1/2 soup cans of water
1/4 teaspoon pepper

Brown beef and onion, **drain**.
Add remaining 7 ingredients to beef mixture.
Place in 9x13 baking dish.
Bake at 350 degrees **covered** for 45 minutes.
Garnish with chinese noodles and **bake** 15 more minutes.

Q: Why did the blonde have blisters on her lips?
A: From trying to blow out lightbulbs.

Crock Pot Cubed Steak

"Blonde Rings"

$^1/_3$ cup flour
6 beef cube steaks
1 Tablespoon oil
1 onion, sliced in rings
3 cups water, divided
1 envelope mushroom gravy mix

Coat cube steak in flour and **brown** both sides in oil.
Place in crock pot.
Add onion rings and 2 cups of water
Cook on low 4-6 hours.
Mix mushroom gravy and 1 cup water together.
Pour in crock pot.
Cook 30 minutes longer.
Serve over rice.

Enchilada Bake

"Not The Same Ole Enchilada"

1 pound ground beef
1 ($4^1/_2$ ounce) can chopped green chilies
2 cans cream of chicken soup
8 corn tortillas, cut into strips
1 pound Velveeta cheese, cubed
16 ounces shredded cheddar cheese

Brown meat and **drain**.
Add next 3 ingredients to meat mixture.
Melt Velveeta cheese and **add** to mixture.
Place in 9x13 baking dish.
Bake at 400 degrees **covered** for 30-35 minutes.
Sprinkle cheese on top of mixture until melted.

Eye-of-Round

"Lazered Eyes"

$1/2$ teaspoon salt
$1/2$ teaspoon pepper
$1/2$ cup Italian dressing
$1/4$ cup steak sauce
1 cup water
1 (3 pound) eye-of-round roast

Combine first 5 ingredients.
Place roast in 9x13 baking dish.
Pour sauce over roast.
Bake at 325 degrees **uncovered** for 2 hours.
Add water occasionally.
Cover and **bake** for 20 more minutes.

Hamburger & Potato

"Hearty Man"

1 pound ground beef, browned, drained
3 potatoes, peeled, diced
3 celery stalks, chopped
1 bell pepper, chopped
1 ($14\frac{1}{2}$ ounce) can diced tomatoes
8 ounces shredded cheddar cheese

Layer first 5 ingredients in 9x13 dish in order given.
Sprinkle each layer with salt and pepper.
Bake at 350 degrees for $1\frac{1}{2}$ hours.
Sprinkle with cheese and **bake** until melted.

Lasagna

"Blonde Italian"

- **1 pound ground beef**
- **1 onion, chopped**
- **1 (14½ ounce) can diced tomatoes**
- **2 (6 ounce) cans tomato paste**
- **1 cup water**
- **8 lasagna noodles**
- **1 (16 ounce) carton ricotta cheese**
- **2 eggs, beaten**
- **8 ounces mozzarella cheese**

Brown beef and onion, **drain**.
Add next 3 ingredients and **simmer** for 30 minute.
Boil noodles according to directions.
Place 4 noodles in 9x13 baking dish.
Combine ricotta and eggs and **spread** over noodles.
Spread meat sauce over ricotta mixture.
Sprinkle ½ mozzarella cheese over meat mixture.
Repeat layers.
Bake at 350 degrees **uncovered** for 35-45 minutes.

Q: Why did the blonde climb up to the roof of the bar?
A: She heard that the drinks were on the house.

Meatball Casserole

"Balls & Meat"

1 pound ground chuck
1 onion, chopped
1/2 teaspoon pepper
1 teaspoon garlic powder
1 teaspoon salt
1/2 cup oatmeal
1 cup milk
1 can cream of mushroom soup
1/2 cup chili sauce

Mix first 6 ingredients together well.
Combine milk and soup and **add** 1/2 to meat mixture.
Shape into balls.
Roll in flour and **brown** in hot oil.
Place meatballs in 2 quart casserole dish.
Add chili sauce to remaining soup mixture.
Pour over meatballs.
Bake at 350 degrees **uncovered** for 45-50 minutes.

Q: Why do blondes work seven days a week?
A: So you don't have to retrain them on Monday.

Meat Loaf

"Gitty-Up Meat"

1 1/2 pounds ground beef
3 slices bread, torn into small pieces
1 egg, beaten
1 (10 ounce) can diced Rotel tomatoes
2 teaspoons chili powder
1/3 cup chili sauce

Combine first 5 ingredients together.
Put in ungreased loaf pan.
Bake at 375 degrees **uncovered** for 1 hour.
Drain excess drippings.
Pour chili sauce over cooked loaf.
Bake 15 more minutes.

Deodorant

A blonde goes into a pharmacy and tells the clerk, "I need some deodorant for my husband." "The ball kind?" inquired the clerk. "No," replied the blonde, "The kind for under his arms."

Pepper Steak

"Spicy Flanked Meat"

$^1/_2$ pound flank steak, cut in thin strips
1 Tablespoon oil
1 envelope dried onion soup mix
$^1/_4$ teaspoon garlic powder
$^1/_2$ teaspoon salt & pepper
1 cup water, divided
1 bell pepper, cut in thin strips
1 tomato, cut in wedges
$1^1/_2$ teaspoon cornstarch

Brown beef in oil and **drain**.
Stir in next 3 ingredients with $^3/_4$ cup water.
Simmer covered for 15 minutes.
Add next 2 ingredients and **simmer covered** for 15 minutes.
Blend cornstarch with $^1/_4$ cup water.
Add to mixture and **bring** to a boil.
Simmer 5 more minutes.
Serve over rice.

Q: How did the blonde die drinking milk?
A: The cow sat down.

Pizza Cups

"Italian Cups"

1 pound ground beef
1 (6 ounce) can tomato paste
1 Tablespoon minced onion
1 teaspoon Italian seasoning
1 (10 count) can biscuits
4 ounces shredded mozzarella cheese

Brown beef and **drain**.
Stir in next 3 ingredients and **cook** over low heat for 5 minutes.
Place each biscuit in greased muffin tins **covering** bottom and sides.
Fill each biscuit with beef mixture.
Sprinkle with cheese.
Bake at 400 degrees for 12 minutes.

Q: What is written at the bottom of a blonde's fishing pond?
A: Bring your own fish.

Rump Roast & More

"Moore Rump for the Roast"

- 1 (3 pound) rump roast
- 1/2 cup flour
- 1 Tablespoon garlic salt
- 2 Tablespoons oil
- 1 envelope dried onion soup mix
- 2 cups water
- 6 potatoes, cubed
- 1/2 pound carrots, sliced
- salt to taste

Cover rump roast in flour, salt.
Pan fry in oil on medium until browned.
Add onion soup mix to water and **boil** for 1 minute.
Put roast in 2 quart casserole dish.
Pour soup mix over roast.
Add cubed potatoes and carrots.
Bake at 350 degrees **covered** for 2 1/2 hours.
Uncover and **bake** 35 more minutes.

Q: Have you heard what my blonde neighbor wrote on the bottom of her swimming pool?
A: No smoking.

Spaghetti Pie

"Bye Bye Miss Italian Pie"

1 pound ground chuck
1/3 cup onion, chopped
1 (26 ounce) jar spaghetti sauce, of choice
1 (7 ounce) spaghetti noodles
2 eggs, beaten
1/4 cup parmesan cheese
1 (8 ounce) sour cream
4 ounces shredded mozzarella cheese
salt & pepper to taste

Brown meat and onion, **drain**.
Stir meat into sauce and **simmer** 10 minutes, **set** aside.
Break spaghetti noodles in half.
Cook noodles according to package and **drain.**
Combine spaghetti noodles with next 3 ingredients.
Pour into greased 10" pie plate.
Spoon sour cream over spaghetti noodles.
Pour meat sauce over noodles.
Bake at 350 degrees for 25 minutes.
Place cheese on top and **return** to oven until melted.

Q: What does a blonde do when someone says its chili outside?
A: She grabs a bowl.

Taco Pizza

"Round Dough"

1 pound ground beef
1 package taco seasoning mix
1 (16 ounce) can refried beans
1 (10 ounce) tube refrigerator pizza dough
2 tomatoes, chopped
8 ounces shredded cheddar cheese

Brown beef and **drain**.
Stir in next 2 ingredients.
Simmer for 10 minutes.
Prepare pizza dough according to directions.
Press onto pizza pan.
Layer with meat mixture, tomatoes and cheese.
Bake at 400 degrees for 8-10 minutes.

Q: How do you sink a submarine full of blondes?
A: Knock on the door.

Barbeque Chicken

"Barby's Qued"

4 boneless, skinless chicken breasts
4 bacon strips, cut in half
1 (9 ounce) bottle honey barbeque sauce
8 ounces shredded cheddar cheese
salt to taste
pepper to taste

Line 9x13 baking dish with foil, overlapping enough to cover chicken.
Place chicken in dish and **sprinkle** with salt and pepper.
Cover each chicken with 2 bacon strip halves.
Top with barbeque sauce and **cover** with foil.
Bake at 350 degrees for 50-60 minutes.
Broil last 10 minutes until bacon is crisp.
Top chicken with cheese and **broil** until melts.

Q: What stops then goes, stops then goes?
A: A blonde at a blinking red light.

Cashew Chicken

"Chick's Cashin In"

- **4 boneless, skinless chicken breasts**
- **1 (14 1/2 ounce) can chicken broth**
- **1/4 cup soy sauce**
- **1 can cream of mushroom soup**
- **1 can cream of chicken soup**
- **1/2 cup cashews, chopped**
- **1 cup rice, cooked**
- **1 (5 ounce) can chow mein noodles**
- **3 green onions, chopped**

Boil chicken for 20 minutes, **drain** and **chop.**
Mix next 5 ingredients with chicken.
Cook rice and **combine** all ingredients.
Place in 9x13 baking dish.
Bake at 350 degrees for 20-25 minutes.
Top with noodles and green onions.
Bake for 5 more minutes.

Q: What do you call 10 blondes standing ear to ear?
A: A wind tunnel.

Chicken Lasagna

"Italian Chick"

- **4 boneless, skinless chicken breasts**
- **1 can cream of chicken soup**
- **1 can cream of mushroom soup**
- **1 (14½ ounce) can chicken broth**
- **¼ teaspoon garlic powder**
- **¼ teaspoon pepper**
- **8 lasagna noodles**
- **3 cups shredded cheddar cheese**
- **8 ounces shredded mozzarella cheese**

Boil chicken breasts for 20 minutes, **drain** and **chop**, **set** aside.
Mix next 5 ingredients together.
Cook noodles and **drain**.
Layer ½ noodles, ½ chicken, ½ soup mixture and ½ cheddar cheese in 9x13 baking dish.
Repeat layers.
Top with mozzarella cheese.
Bake at 350 degrees **covered** for 50-60 minutes.

Q: What do you call two blondes in the freezer?
A: Frosted flakes.

Chicken Pie

"Easy Chick"

2 boneless, skinless chicken breasts
1/2 cup chopped onion
1 stick margarine
1 (8 ounce) sour cream
1 can cream of chicken soup
2 (9 inch) pie shells, unbaked

Boil chicken breasts for 20 minutes, **drain** and **chop**, **set** aside.
Sauté onion in margarine.
Mix all ingredients together.
Place in pie shell.
Put other pie shell on top, and seal edges.
Bake at 375 degrees **uncovered** for 45-50 minutes.

Chicken Roll-Ups

"Roll Me Chick"

2 boneless, skinless chicken breasts
1/2 cup sour cream
4 green onions, chopped
16 ounces shredded mozzarella cheese
1 (8 ounce) can crescent rolls
1 splash lemon juice

Boil chicken breasts for 20 minutes, **drain** and **chop**.
Mix next 4 ingredients with chicken.
Spread rolls out in triangles, **put** mixture in, and **seal**.
Place on cookie sheet.
Bake at 350 degrees **uncovered** for 20-30 minutes.

Chicken Spaghetti

"Limpy Chick"

4 boneless, skinless chicken breasts
1 stick margarine
1 bell pepper, chopped
1 onion, chopped
1 (16 ounce) package spaghetti noodles
1 pound Velveeta cheese
1 (10 ounce) can diced Rotel tomatoes
1 (8.5 ounce) can English peas
1 can cream of mushroom soup

Boil chicken breasts for 20 minutes, **drain** and **chop**.
Sauté pepper and onion in butter.
Boil noodles according to directions.
Melt cheese in microwave for 2-3 minutes.
Combine all ingredients together.
Put in 9x13 baking dish.
Bake at 350 degrees **covered** for 50-60 minutes.

Q: Why do blondes always rapidly flap their hands towards theirs ears?
A: They're refueling.

Chinese Chicken

"Asian Chick"

4 boneless, skinless chicken breasts
3 Tablespoons oil
1 (8 ounce) can bamboo shoots
1 (8 ounce) sliced fresh mushrooms
2 cups bean sprouts
2 (8 ounce) cans sliced water chestnuts
4 Tablespoons lemon juice
4 Tablespoons sesame seeds
2 cups rice, cooked

Boil chicken breasts for 20 minutes, **drain** and **chop**.
Combine chicken with next 7 ingredients.
Sauté for 8 minutes.
Serve over rice.

Crock Pot Chicken

"Slow and Easy"

4 boneless, skinless chicken breasts
1 teaspoon salt
1 teaspoon garlic salt
1 teaspoon pepper
1 can cream of mushroom soup
1 can cream of chicken soup
1 Tablespoon minced onion
1 (7 ounce) can mushroom pieces & stems
1 bell pepper, cut in strips

Place all ingredients in crock pot.
Cook on high for 3-4 hours or low all day.

Dried Beef Chicken

"P-A-R-T-Y H-A-R-D-Y Chick"

1 (2.25 ounce) jar dried beef
8 boneless, skinless chicken breasts
8 bacon strips
1 can cream of mushroom soup
1 (8 ounce) sour cream
salt and pepper to taste

Place dried beef in 9x13 baking dish.
Wrap each breast with a strip of bacon.
Arrange chicken on dried beef.
Mix last 3 ingredients.
Pour over chicken.
Bake 350 degrees **uncovered** for 1 hour.

Lemon Chicken

"Sour Puss Chick"

6 boneless, skinless chicken breasts
1/2 cup oil
1/2 cup lemon juice
1 can cream of chicken soup
1/2 teaspoon salt
1/2 teaspoon pepper

Place chicken in 9x13 baking dish.
Mix next 5 ingredients and **pour** over chicken.
Bake at 350 degrees **covered** for 1 hour.
Uncover and **bake** 10 minutes longer.

Mexican Chicken
"Ranchero Chick"

4 boneless, skinless chicken breasts
1 can cream of mushroom soup
1 can cream of chicken soup
1 (10 ounce) can mild enchilada sauce
12 ounces shredded cheddar cheese
1 (15 ounce) bag plain tortilla chips

Boil chicken breasts for 20 minutes, **drain** and **chop**.
Mix all ingredients together.
Place in 9x13 baking dish.
Bake at 350 degrees **covered** for 1 hour.

Poppy Seed Chicken
"Eye Poppin' Chick"

8 boneless, skinless chicken breasts
1 (16 ounce) sour cream
2 cans cream of chicken soup
2 Tablespoons poppy seeds
3 sleeves Ritz crackers, crushed
1 1/2 Tablespoons margarine

Boil chicken breasts for 20 minutes, **drain** and **chop**.
Mix next 3 ingredients together.
Layer chicken, soup mixture, crackers in 9x13 baking dish.
Melt margarine and **pour** over top.
Bake at 350 degrees **uncovered** for 1 hour.
Serve over rice.

Russian Chicken Breasts

"Rushin' Breasts"

8 boneless, skinless chicken breasts
1 (10 ounce) jar peach or apricot marmalade
1 (8 ounce) bottle Catalina dressing
1 package dry onion soup mix
salt to taste
pepper to taste

Season chicken with salt and pepper.
Combine rest of ingredients and **mix** well.
Layer half sauce on bottom of 9x13 baking dish.
Place chicken on top.
Pour remaining sauce over chicken.
Marinate overnight or for 5 hours.
Bake at 325 degrees **uncovered** for 1 hour.

Q: Why do blondes comb their bangs straight up?
A: Because they don't want anything going over their head.

Wild Rice & Chicken

"Wild Chick"

- **3 boneless, skinless chicken breasts**
- **1 (6 ounce) box long grain wild rice**
- **2 Tablespoons margarine**
- **1 teaspoon Worcestershire**
- **1 teaspoon flour**
- **1 cup milk**
- **4 ounces shredded cheddar cheese**
- **2 Tablespoons red wine**
- **salt and pepper to taste**

Boil chicken breasts for 20 minutes, **drain** and **chop**.
Cook rice according to package.
Sauté next 4 ingredients in saucepan until thick.
Add remaining ingredients.
Combine all ingredients together.
Bake at 350 degrees **covered** for 25-30 minutes.

Windows

A blonde girl enters a store that sells curtains. She tells the salesman, "I would like to buy a pink curtain for my computer screen."

The surprised salesman replied … "But madam, computers do not have curtains."!!

And the blonde said, "Hello …… I've got WINDOWS."

Boneless Pork Butterflies

"Fly Away with me"

8 boneless pork butterfly chops
2 eggs, beaten
1/2 cup Italian breadcrumbs
1/2 cup parmesan cheese
2 Tablespoons olive oil
salt and pepper to taste

Dip pork chops in eggs.
Combine next 4 ingredients and **dip** chops in mixture.
Put in skillet and pan **fry** in olive oil for 40 minutes.
Turn occasionally.

Coke Pork Chops

"Ham's Addiction"

8 pork chops
1/4 teaspoon salt
1/4 teaspoon pepper
1 cup ketchup
1 cup Coke
1/4 cup brown sugar

Place pork chops in 9x13 baking dish.
Sprinkle with salt and pepper.
Mix ketchup and Coke.
Pour over chops.
Sprinkle with brown sugar.
Bake at 350 degrees **uncovered** for 1 hour.

Country Glazed Ham

"He's a Little Bit Country"

- **1 (10 pound) half ham with bone-in**
- **1/2 cup Dijon mustard**
- **1/2 cup sherry**
- **1/2 cup honey**
- **3/4 cup brown sugar**
- **1/4 cup white sugar**

Wrap ham in foil.
Bake at 350 degrees in 9x13 dish for 2 hours.
Combine next 5 ingredients in saucepan.
Unwrap ham, **trim** off fat and **pour** off excess liquid.
Pour glaze over ham and **cook** additional hour on 325 degrees.
Reapplying sauce every 15 minutes.

Easy Pork Chops

"French Blonde"

- **5 potatoes, peeled, sliced**
- **5 pork chops**
- **1 can cheddar cheese soup**
- **1 can French onion soup**
- **1/2 teaspoon salt**
- **1/2 teaspoon pepper**

Place potatoes in 9x13 baking dish.
Place chops over potatoes.
Combine remaining ingredients.
Pour over chops and **cover** with aluminum foil.
Bake at 350 degrees for 1 hour.

Ham and Potatoes

"Pork Luck"

8 ounces shredded swiss cheese
1/2 onion, finely chopped
1/2 stick margarine
2 Tablespoons flour
2 cups milk
1/2 teaspoon salt
6 potatoes, peeled, diced
3 cups ham, diced
1 cup breadcrumbs

Mix cheese and onions and **set** aside.
Combine next four ingredients in saucepan.
Cook over medium heat until thick and smooth
Layer 1/2 potatoes, 1/2 cheese, 1/2 sauce, 1/2 ham in 9x13 inch dish.
Repeat layers.
Sprinkle breadcrumbs on top of mixture.
Bake at 350 degrees **covered** for 1 hour.

Q: Did you hear about the dead blonde in the closet?
A: She was last year's hide and seek winner.

Lemon Barbecue Pork Chops

"Pucker Up Your Chops"

2 Tablespoons green onions, chopped
1 Tablespoon margarine
1/2 cup ketchup
1/4 cup soy sauce
1 Tablespoon lemon juice
2 Tablespoons brown sugar
2 Tablespoons white wine
salt and pepper to taste
6 pork chops

Sauté onions in margarine.
Stir in next 6 ingredients and **simmer**.
Place pork chops on grill and **brush** with sauce.
Baste and **turn** every 10 minutes, **cooking** for 30 minutes.

Q: Why did the blonde purchase an AM radio?
A: She didn't want one for nights.

Orange Glazed Spare Ribs

"Make His Eyes Glaze"

4 pounds spare ribs
1 (16 ounce) can frozen orange juice, thawed
1½ teaspoons Worcestershire
½ teaspoon garlic salt
⅛ teaspoon pepper
⅛ teaspoon cayenne pepper

Cut ribs into serving pieces and **place** in large saucepan.
Add water to cover ribs, **bring** to a boil.
Cover, **reduce** heat and **simmer** for 1 hour.
Drain and **place** in large shallow roasting pan, **set** aside.
Combine last 5 ingredients.
Brush on ribs.
Bake at 325 degrees **uncovered** for 30-45 minutes.

Party Pork Loin

"Partying On North State"

1 (3 pound) boneless pork loin
3 bacon strips
1 can cream of mushroom soup
1 can cream of chicken soup
¼ cup Dijon mustard
1 (8 ounce) sour cream

Wrap pork loin with bacon strips.
Combine next 4 ingredients and **pour** over pork.
Cover with foil and **bake** at 300 degrees for 3 hours.
Broil last 15 minutes for crispy bacon.
Serve over rice.

Pork Parmesan

"Fake Him Off"

- **6 boneless pork chops**
- **3 eggs, beaten**
- **1 1/2 cups Italian breadcrumbs**
- **1 (8 ounce) can tomato sauce**
- **16 ounces shredded mozzarella cheese**
- **cooking oil**

Dip pork chops in egg, **roll** in crumbs.
Brown chops in cooking oil.
Place pork in 9 x13 baking dish.
Pour tomato sauce on each chop.
Sprinkle with cheese.
Bake at 350 degrees **covered** for 50 minutes.

Q: If a blonde and a brunette are tossed off a building, who hits the ground first?
A: The brunette. The blonde has to stop to ask directions.

Sausage Spinach Pie

"Blondes Taking the Green Back"

1 pound sausage, browned
6 eggs, beaten
1 (10 ounce) package frozen chopped spinach, thawed & drained
1 cup ricotta cheese
16 ounces shredded mozzarella cheese
1 clove garlic, minced
1/2 teaspoon salt
1/4 teaspoon pepper
4 (9 inch) pie shells

Combine first 8 ingredients together.
Put mixture into 2 pie shells.
Top each pie shell with extra shell.
Pinch edges together and **cut** 4 slits in top.
Bake at 350 degrees **uncovered** for 40-50 minutes.

Baked Catfish

"Delta Retzie"

6 catfish filets
1 Tablespoon liquid smoke
1 teaspoon garlic juice
1/2 stick margarine, melted
1/3 cup soy sauce
1/2 teaspoon salt

Place catfish in foil.
Combine remaining ingredients and **brush** over catfish.
Wrap in foil.
Bake at 400 degrees for 30 minutes.

Crab Cakes

"It's All In The Crabs"

1 stick margarine
1/4 cup flour
2 cups milk
2 eggs, beaten
1 pound lump crabmeat
2 sleeves saltine crackers, finely crushed
1 cup breadcrumbs
2 Tablespoons creole seasoning
1/2 teaspoon cayenne pepper

Mix first 2 ingredients and **cook** 3 minutes.
Slowly add milk, **stirring** until thickened.
Combine egg and crabmeat in mixing bowl.
Fold milk gently into mixture.
Divide mixture into 3 ounce patties.
Combine last 4 ingredients in a separate bowl.
Dip patties in breadcrumb mixture.
Sauté patties in oil until lightly brown.
Put in baking dish.
Bake at 350 degrees for 5-8 minutes.

Q: Why are there blonde jokes?
A: To make brunettes jealous.

Feta Shrimp Pasta

"Golden Greek"

- **1/4 cup olive oil**
- **2 garlic cloves, crushed**
- **6 roma tomatoes, cut in strips**
- **1/2 cup Greek black olives**
- **1 (16 ounce) package fettuccini**
- **2 pounds shrimp, cooked**
- **8 ounces feta cheese, crumbled**
- **1/2 cup basil**
- **1/4 cup parmesan cheese**

Sauté garlic in olive oil.
Add next 2 ingredients, **cook** for 3 minutes.
Combine garlic with tomato and olives, **keep** warm.
Cook fettuccini, according to directions.
Toss feta, basil and parmesan cheese with shrimp.
Toss all ingredients together.

Q: What's the advantage of being married to a blonde?
A: You can park in the handicapped zone.

Mexican Shrimp Pasta

"South Of The Border"

- **1 onion**
- **2 Tablespoons olive oil**
- **3 (14 1/2 ounce) cans diced tomatoes**
- **1/2 cup picante sauce**
- **1 teaspoon basil**
- **1 teaspoon oregano**
- **1 pound shrimp, raw, peeled**
- **1 bell pepper, sliced**
- **16 ounces linguine, cooked**

Sauté onion in olive oil in saucepan.
Add next 4 ingredients.
Bring to a boil and **simmer** for 10 minutes.
Add shrimp and bell pepper, **simmer** for 10 minutes.
Toss linguine with shrimp mixture.

Overhead

A blonde was walking along when she looked up to observe a bird flying overhead. Suddenly, the bird drops a load directly over her. The blonde says, "Good thing I had my mouth open, or that would've hit me right in the face!"

Oyster Pie

"Aphrodisiac"

2 potatoes, peeled, diced
2 celery stalks, chopped
2 carrots, sliced
salt to taste
pepper to taste
1 pint oysters
9 inch pie shell
1/2 stick margarine
1/2 cup milk, heated

Boil first 3 ingredients until tender.
Put salt and pepper on vegetables.
Layer vegetables and oysters in pie shell.
Slice margarine and **put** on oysters.
Pour milk over oysters.
Bake at 375 degrees for 35 minutes.

Q: What do you call a blonde with a brand new P.C.?
A: A dumb terminal.

Seafood Casserole

"Destiny Divine"

- **1 stick margarine**
- **1 onion, chopped**
- **1 bell pepper, chopped**
- **8 ounces fresh sliced mushrooms**
- **1 (8 ounce) cream cheese, softened**
- **1 can cream of mushroom soup**
- **1 teaspoon salt**
- **2 pounds favorite seafood, cooked, peeled**
- **4 cups rice, cooked**

Sauté first 4 ingredients until lightly brown.
Cream next 3 ingredients with vegetables.
Combine your favorite seafood with mixture.
Pour in 9x13 dish.
Bake at 350 degrees for 30-40 minutes.
Serve over rice.

Q: How do you call a blonde?
A: You don't .... you whistle.

Shrimp Pasta
"Limp Shrimp"

1 (16 ounce) package Angel hair pasta
1 bell pepper, chopped
1 stick margarine
1 (10 ounce) can diced Rotel tomatoes
2 teaspoons oregano
2 teaspoons basil
2 Tablespoons lemon juice
1 (16 ounce) can evaporated milk
2 pounds shrimp, cooked, peeled

Cook pasta according to directions and **set** aside.
Sauté bell pepper in margarine.
Combine next 4 ingredients with pepper.
Cook on medium heat for 20 minutes.
Add milk, **cook** for 10-15 minutes.
Add shrimp, **cook** for 10-15 more minutes.
Serve over pasta.

Q: What does a blonde say when she see's a banana skin on the side walk?
A: Am I going to fall again!!!!!!!

Shrimp Quiche

"Real Men Do Quiche"

2	**eggs, beaten**
1/2	**cup milk**
1/2	**cup half & half cream**
1/2	**teaspoon salt**
1/2	**teaspoon pepper**
	dash of cayenne
3/4	**pound shrimp, cooked, diced**
8	**ounces shredded swiss cheese**
1	**(9 inch) pie shell**

Combine first 6 ingredients together.
Put shrimp and cheese in pie shell.
Pour egg mixture over shrimp.
Bake at 400 degrees for 30 minutes.

Q: What happens when a blonde gets Alzheimers disease?
A: Her IQ goes up!

Shrimp Spaghetti

"Blonde Shrimp"

- **16 ounces spaghetti, cooked**
- **8 ounces Velveeta cheese, melted**
- **1 (10 ounce) can diced Rotel tomatoes**
- **2 pounds shrimp, uncooked, peeled**
- **1 stick margarine, melted**
- **2 Tablespoons Italian seasoning**
- **1 Tablespoon Worcestershire**
- **1 Tablespoon lemon juice**
- **1/2 teaspoon basil**

Mix all ingredients together in large bowl.
Bake at 350 degrees for 45 minutes.

Tangy Snapper

"Don't Let Him Snap"

- **1 1/2 cups orange juice**
- **1/2 cup lime juice**
- **1/2 cup honey**
- **2 pounds snapper filets, scored**
- **2 teaspoons paprika**
- **1 teaspoon salt**

Combine first 3 ingredients together.
Pour over filets and **marinate** in refrigerator for an hour.
Take filets out of marinade and **add** last 2 ingredients.
Broil 10 minutes for each inch of thickness.
Heat marinade in saucepan for 5 minutes.
Pour over filets and **broil** until fish flakes off of fork.

Happy Endings

(Cakes, Cookies, Desserts & Pies)

Happy Endings
(Cakes, Cookies, Pies & Sweets)

Cakes

Cookies

Pies

Sweets

Apple Cake
"Adam Or Evie"

3 eggs
1 1/4 cups oil
2 cups sugar
2 1/2 cups self-rising flour
2 apples, peeled, finely chopped
1 (7 ounce) bag coconut

Mix all ingredients together.
Pour into greased bundt pan.
Bake at 350 degrees for 1 hour.

Cappuccino Cake
"Wake Him Up"

1 (6 ounce) bag chocolate chips
1/2 cup pecans, chopped
1 box yellow cake mix
4 Tablespoons instant espresso coffee powder
2 teaspoons cinnamon
1/3 cup olive oil
3 eggs
1 1/4 cups water
powdered sugar

Combine first 2 ingredients, **pour** into greased bundt pan.
Mix next 6 ingredients together in order.
Pour batter over chips and nuts.
Bake at 325 degrees for 50-60 minutes.
Sprinkle with powdered sugar.

Carrot Cake

"What's Up Doc"

- **1 box yellow cake mix**
- **4 eggs**
- **1 1/4 cups oil**
- **1/4 cup cold water**
- **2 teaspoons cinnamon**
- **2 cups carrots, grated**

Mix all ingredients together in order.
Pour into 2 greased 9 inch pans.
Bake at 350 degrees for 30-35 minutes.

Cream Cheese Icing:

- **1 stick margarine, softened**
- **1 (16 ounce) box powdered sugar**
- **2 teaspoons vanilla extract**
- **1 (8 ounce) cream cheese, softened**
- **1/4 teaspoon salt**
- **1 cup pecans, chopped**

Combine all ingredients together.
Ice each cake and then **layer**.

Q: How many blonde jokes are there?
A: None, they're all true.

Banana Split Cake

"Split it with Me"

3 sticks margarine, softened
2 cups graham cracker crumbs
1 (16 ounce) box powdered sugar
2 eggs
5-7 bananas, sliced
1 (8 ounce) can crushed pineapple, drained
1 cup pecans, chopped
1 (12 ounce) Cool Whip
1 jar of cherries

Blend 1 stick margarine with cracker crumbs.
Pat into bottom of 9x13 pan.
Beat 2 sticks margarine, sugar and eggs.
Spread over crust.
Layer next 4 ingredients.
Chill for 2 hours.
Top with cherries.

Q: What do you get when you offer a blonde a penny for her thoughts?
A: Change.

Chocolate Chip Cake

"Angels In Heaven"

- **1 box yellow cake mix**
- **1 (3 ounce) box instant vanilla pudding**
- **1 (3 ounce) box instant chocolate pudding**
- **4 eggs**
- **1 Tablespoon vanilla extract**
- **1 (8 ounce) sour cream**
- **1 cup oil**
- **1/4 cup water**
- **1 (6 ounce) bag chocolate chips**

Mix all ingredients together, **beat** until smooth.
Pour batter into greased bundt pan.
Bake at 325 degrees for 50-60 minutes.

New Tech

A blonde says to her psychiatrist, "I'm on the road a lot, and my clients are complaining that they can never reach me." He replies, "Don't you have a phone in your car?" She says, "That was a little too expensive, so I did the next best thing. I put a mailbox in my car." The psychiatrist, laughing to himself, asks, "Uh, how's that working?" The blonde replies, "Actually, I haven't gotten any letters yet." He asks, "and why do you think that is?" The blonde in all her wisdom replies, "I figure it's because when I'm driving around my post code keeps changing."

Coconut Cake

"Casper's Flaky"

1 box yellow cake mix

Frosting:

1 (16 ounce) sour cream, divided
1 cup sugar
1 teaspoon vanilla extract
2 (7 ounce) bags coconut
1 (8 ounce) Cool Whip

Bake cake in 2 round greased cake pans as directed on box.
Cool and **slice** each cake in half to make 4 thin layers.
Combine 1 cup sour cream, sugar, vanilla and 1 bag coconut
Spread between each layer.
Combine 1 cup sour cream and Cool Whip.
Spread on top and sides of entire cake.
Sprinkle with remaining coconut.
Place in airtight container and **refrigerate** for 2-3 days.

Q: How did the blonde burn her ear?
A: The phone rang while she was ironing.

Italian Cream Cake

"He's Worth It"

1 box French vanilla cake mix
3 eggs, separated
1 stick margarine, melted
1/2 teaspoon baking soda
1/2 teaspoon water
1 teaspoon vanilla extract
1 cup buttermilk
1 cup coconut
1/2 cup pecans, chopped

Mix cake mix, egg yolks, and margarine together.
Add next 6 ingredients.
Beat egg whites, **fold** into cake mixture.
Pour into three greased 9 inch pans.
Bake at 350 degrees for 30-40 minutes.
Layer and **ice** with cream cheese icing. **See** Carrot Cake for icing.

Lemonade Cake

"Sweet Tart"

1 box lemon cake mix
1 (3 ounce) box lemon instant pudding
4 eggs
1 cup water
1/4 cup oil
1 teaspoon vanilla extract

Mix all ingredients together.
Pour into greased bundt pan.
Bake at 350 for 1 hour.

Pina Colada Cake

"Tropical Blonde"

- **1 box pineapple cake mix**
- **$1\frac{1}{4}$ cups pineapple juice**
- **1 (14 ounce) can condensed milk**
- **1 (8 ounce) Cool Whip**
- **1 (7 ounce) bag coconut**
- **1 (8 ounce) can cream of coconut**

Make cake according to directions. (**Use** pineapple juice instead of water.)
Pour into greased 9x13 dish and **bake** as directed.
Punch holes in cake while hot.
Mix together rest of ingredients.
Pour over cake and **cool**.
Keep refrigerated.

Butter Cream Cheese Pound Cake

"Pound On Him"

- **3 sticks butter, softened**
- **1 (8 ounce) cream cheese, softened**
- **3 cups sugar**
- **5 eggs**
- **2 teaspoons vanilla extract**
- **3 cups all-purpose flour**

Mix all ingredients together in order.
Pour into greased bundt pan.
Bake at 325 degrees for $1\frac{1}{2}$ hours.

Chocolate Pound Cake

"Chocolate By The Pound"

- **2 sticks butter, softened**
- **2 cups sugar**
- **5 eggs**
- **1/2 cup cocoa**
- **3 cups self-rising flour**
- **1 cup buttermilk**

Cream butter and sugar together.
Add remaining ingredients.
Pour into greased bundt pan.
Bake for 1 1/2 hours.

ICING:

- **2 cups sugar**
- **1/4 cup milk**
- **1/4 cup cocoa**
- **1/4 cup evaporated milk**
- **1/4 cup karo syrup**
- **1 teaspoon vanilla extract**

Mix first 5 ingredients together, **boil** for 1 minute.
Add vanilla and **beat** until ready to spread on cake.

Q: Why do blondes wear their hair up?
A: To catch anything that goes over their heads.

Punch Bowl Cake

"He Loves Me Not"

- **1 box yellow cake mix**
- **2 (3 ounce) boxes instant vanilla pudding**
- **1 quart strawberries, sliced**
- **1 (20 ounce) can crushed pineapple**
- **1 (7 ounce) bag coconut**
- **1 (12 ounce) Cool Whip**

Bake cake in 2 round greased cake pans according to directions.
Make pudding according to directions.
Crumble 1 layer of cake in bottom of punch bowl.
Layer 1/2 pudding mix, 1/2 strawberries, 1/2 pineapples, 1/2 coconut, 1/2 Cool Whip.
Crumble second cake over ingredients.
Layer with other half of ingredients.

Red Velvet Cake

"Remember Me"

- **1 box German chocolate cake mix**
- **1 bottle red food coloring**
- **1 Tablespoon instant coffee crystals**
- **3 eggs**
- **1/2 cup oil**
- **1 1/4 cups water**

Mix all ingredients together.
Pour into 2 greased round cake pans.
Bake at 350 degrees for 25-30 minutes.
Frost with cream cheese icing. **See** Carrot Cake for icing.

Strawberry Cake

"Not A Strawberry Blonde"

- **1 box white cake mix**
- **1 (3 ounce) box strawberry jello**
- **1/4 cup water**
- **4 eggs, beaten**
- **1 cup oil**
- **1 (10 ounce) box frozen strawberries, thawed, divided in half**
- **1 stick margarine, softened**
- **1 (16 ounce) box powdered sugar**
- **1 teaspoon vanilla extract**

Mix first 5 ingredients together.
Add 1/2 of strawberries.
Pour into 2 greased round cake pans.
Bake at 350 degrees for 30-40 minutes.
Combine last 3 ingredients together with remaining strawberries.
Ice cake.

Q: Why does a blonde smile when there is lightening?
A: She thinks she is getting her picture taken.

Turtle Cake

"He Takes His Time"

- **1 box German chocolate cake mix**
- **1 (12 ounce) jar caramel topping**
- **2 sticks margarine, softened**
- **1/2 cup evaporated milk**
- **1 (6 ounce) bag chocolate chips**
- **1 cup pecans**

Mix cake according to directions.
Pour 1/2 of batter into greased 9x13 pan.
Mix next 3 ingredients together.
Pour caramel mixture over 1/2 cake batter.
Sprinkle chocolate chips and pecans over batter.
Top with other half of batter.
Bake at 350 degrees for 30-40 minutes.

Q: What do you call a blonde with half a brain?
A: Gifted!

Butterscotch Cookies

"Butter Him Up With Scotch"

1 (6 ounce) bag butterscotch chips
2 sticks margarine, softened
2 Tablespoons boiling water
1 cup self-rising flour
3/4 cup sugar
2 cups oatmeal

Melt butterscotch chips in microwave for 2 minutes.
Mix rest of ingredients in order, **stirring** each time.
Add melted butterscotch chips.
Drop by tablespoon on ungreased cookie sheet.
Bake at 350 degrees for 10-12 minutes.

Chocolate Chip Cookies

"Chippin' Away At His Heart"

1 box yellow cake mix
2 eggs, beaten
1/2 cup oil
1 Tablespoon vanilla extract
1 Tablespoon butter flavoring
1 (12 ounce) bag chocolate chips

Mix all ingredients together.
Drop by tablespoon on ungreased cookie sheet.
Bake at 350 degrees for 8-10 minutes.

Mint Chocolate Chip Cookies

"All Night Kisses"

- **3 egg whites**
- **1/4 teaspoon cream of tartar**
- **1/4 teaspoon salt**
- **1 cup sugar**
- **1 teaspoon vanilla extract**
- **1 (6 ounce) bag mint chocolate chips**

Pre-heat oven to 350 degrees.
Beat first 3 ingredients until stiff.
Add sugar slowly until stiff and shiny.
Add vanilla and mint chips.
Drop by tablespoon onto ungreased cookie sheet.
Put cookies in oven, **turn** off oven.
Leave overnight.
Cookies will **cook** while you sleep.

Q: How do you drown a blonde?
A: Glue a penny to the bottom of a pool.

Cookie Dough Cookies

"Show Me The Dough"

1 (18 ounce) sugar cookie dough roll
1 (6 ounce) bag chocolate chips
1 (12 ounce) jar caramel topping
1/2 cup half & half cream
1 teaspoon vanilla extract
1/2 cup pecans, chopped

Press cookie dough into 9x13 pan.
Bake according to cookie dough directions.
Sprinkle with chocolate chips, **bake** for 5 more minutes.
Heat next 3 ingredients in separate pan until creamy.
Pour over chocolate chips.
Sprinkle with pecans.
Cool and **cut** into bars.

Q: How do blonde brain cells die?
A: Alone.

Lemon Almond Cookies

"All Men Are Sour"

1 box lemon cake mix
1 cup Rice Krispies cereal
1 egg, beaten
1 stick margarine, melted
1 teaspoon lemon juice
1/2 cup chopped almonds

Mix all ingredients together.
Shape into bite-size balls.
Place 2 inches apart on an ungreased cookie sheet.
Bake at 350 degrees for 10-12 minutes.

No Bake Cookies

"More Time To Play"

2 cups sugar
1/2 cup milk
1 stick margarine
3 cups oatmeal
3/4 cup peanut butter, crunchy
1 teaspoon vanilla extract

Boil first 3 ingredients in saucepan for 2 minutes.
Add remaining ingredients.
Mix together, **spoon** onto wax paper.

Oatmeal Cookies

"Old Fashioned Blonde"

1 box yellow cake mix
2 eggs
1 cup sugar
1 cup oil
1 teaspoon vanilla extract
2 cups oatmeal

Mix all ingredients together.
Drop by tablespoon on ungreased cookie sheet.
Bake at 325 degrees for 10-15 minutes.

Peanut Butter Cookies

"Stickin' To Your Roof"

2 sticks margarine, softened
1 cup sugar
1/2 cup brown sugar
3 eggs
2 cups self-rising flour
2 (12 ounce) bags peanut butter chips

Mix all ingredients together.
Drop by tablespoon on ungreased cookie sheet.
Bake at 350 degrees for 10-12 minutes.

Q: Why are there no brunette jokes?
A: Because blondes would have to think them up.

Potato Chip Cookies

"Legally Blonde"

2 sticks margarine, softened
1/2 cup sugar
1 teaspoon vanilla extract
1 3/4 cups self-rising flour
1/2 cup potato chips, crushed
1/2 cup pecans, chopped

Mix all ingredients together in order.
Form into bite-size balls, **put** on ungreased cooked sheet.
Press down with a fork.
Bake at 350 degrees for 12-14 minutes.

Sugar Cookies

"Sweet Talkin'"

3 cups self-rising flour
2 sticks margarine, softened
3 eggs
2 cups sugar
1/4 cup water
2 teaspoons vanilla extract

Mix all ingredients together.
Drop by tablespoon on ungreased cookie sheet.
Set for 10 minutes before baking.
Bake at 350 degrees for 12-15 minutes.

Apple Pie

"Apple Of His Eye"

- **1/2 cup sugar**
- **1/2 cup self-rising flour**
- **1 Tablespoon cinnamon**
- **2 Granny Smith apples, peeled & sliced**
- **1/2 stick margarine, slice**
- **2 pie crust (refrigerated boxed)**

Mix first 3 ingredients in a bowl.
Place 1 apple in pie shell.
Sprinkle 1/2 sugar mixture over apples.
Repeat layers.
Place sliced margarine pieces over sugar mixture.
Cover with other pie crust.
Bake at 350 for 35 minutes.

Buttermilk Pie

"Milking Me Dry"

- **1 1/2 cups sugar**
- **1/2 cup self-rising flour**
- **1 stick margarine, softened**
- **2 eggs, beaten**
- **1 cup buttermilk**
- **1 (9 inch) pie shell, unbaked**

Mix first 5 ingredients together.
Pour in pie shell.
Bake at 350 for 40-45 minutes.

Caramel Coconut Pie

"Blonde Flake"

2 (9 inch) pie shells
1/2 stick margarine
1 (7 ounce) bag coconut
1 cup pecans, chopped
1 teaspoon vanilla extract
1 (3 ounce) cream cheese, softened
1 (14 ounce) can condensed milk
1 (12 ounce) Cool Whip
1 (12 ounce) jar caramel topping

Bake pie shells according to directions.
Add next 4 ingredients in skillet and **brown** lightly.
Combine next 3 ingredients in separate bowl.
Layer 1/4 cream cheese mixture in pie shell.
Drizzle 1/4 caramel topping over cream cheese mixture.
Sprinkle 1/4 of coconut mixture on top.
Repeat layers.
Freeze and **serve** frozen.

Q: What do you call it when a blonde dies their hair brunette?
A: Artificial intelligence.

Easy Cheese Cake

"Dacker Smacker"

3 (8 ounce) cream cheese, softened
1 (14 ounce) can condensed milk
4 eggs
2 teaspoons vanilla extract
1 Tablespoon lemon juice
2 (9 inch) graham cracker crusts

Mix first 5 ingredients together.
Pour into crusts.
Bake at 325 degrees for 50-60 minutes.

Chocolate Chess Pie

"Dark Chest"

1 (9 inch) pie shell, unbaked
1 (6 ounce) bag chocolate chips
1 stick margarine, softened
1 cup sugar
2 eggs
1/2 cup self-rising flour

Put chips in bottom of pie shell.
Mix next 4 ingredients.
Pour mixture into pie shell.
Bake at 350 degrees for 40-45 minutes.

Chocolate Chip Toll House Pie

"PMSing"

2 cups sugar; 1 white & 1 brown sugar
1 cup self-rising flour
2 eggs, beaten
2 sticks margarine, melted
1 (6 ounce) bag chocolate chips
1 (9 inch) pie shell, unbaked

Mix first 5 ingredients together.
Fold in chocolate chips.
Pour into pie shell.
Bake at 325 degrees for 50-60 minutes.

Hershey Bar Pie

"She Is A Her"

6 (1.35 ounce) Hershey bars with almonds
22 large marshmallows
1/2 cup milk
1/4 teaspoon vanilla extract
1/2 cup Cool Whip
1 (9 inch) graham cracker crust

Melt first 4 ingredients in top of double boiler.
Set out to cool.
Fold Cool Whip into mixture.
Pour into crust and **refrigerate**.

Key Lime Pie

"Billy Bob's Tarty"

- **1 (9 inch) pie shell**
- **2 (8 ounce) cream cheese, softened**
- **2 (14 ounce) cans condensed milk**
- **3/4 cup key lime juice, bottled or fresh**
- **1 cup heavy whipping cream**
- **3 Tablespoons powdered sugar**

Bake pie shell according to directions.
Mix next 3 ingredients together.
Pour into pie shell.
Refrigerate for 3 hours.
Mix cream and sugar until stiff peaks are formed.
Refrigerate topping for 2 hours.
Pour on pie.

Lemon Pie

"Pucker Up Hot Lips"

- **1 (14 ounce) can condensed milk**
- **1 teaspoon lemon rind**
- **1/2 cup lemon juice**
- **2 egg yolks**
- **1 (8 ounce) Cool Whip**
- **1 (9 inch) graham cracker crust**

Combine first 5 ingredients together.
Pour into crust, **chill** before serving.

Mandarin Orange Pie

"Orange You Glad He Stayed"

- **2 (11 ounce) cans mandarin oranges**
- **1 (14 ounce) can condensed milk**
- **1 (8 ounce) Cool Whip, thawed**
- **1/8 teaspoon vanilla extract**
- **1 Tablespoon lemon juice**
- **2 (9 inch) graham cracker crusts**

Drain oranges.
Mix next 4 ingredients in with oranges.
Pour into crusts, **refrigerate**.

Margarita Pie

"Tequila Shooter"

- **6 eggs, separated**
- **2 (14 ounce) cans condensed milk**
- **1/2 cup tequila**
- **1/2 cup triple sec**
- **1/2 cup lime juice**
- **1 (9 inch) graham cracker crust**

Combine yolks and condensed milk together.
Combine next 3 ingredients in saucepan.
Simmer for 2 minutes.
Refrigerate tequila mixture for 15 minutes.
Fold egg whites into yolk mixture.
Add tequila mixture.
Pour into crust, **bake** at 325 degrees for 20-25 minutes.

Mystery Pie

"She's Always A Mystery"

1 cup Ritz crackers, crushed
1 cup pecans, chopped
1 cup sugar
1 Tablespoon vanilla extract
1/2 Tablespoon baking soda
4 egg whites

Mix first 5 ingredients together.
Fold in egg whites, beat until stiff.
Pour into greased pie pan.
Bake at 350 degrees for 20 minutes.
Refrigerate overnight and **serve** with Cool Whip.

Oreo Pie

"Creamed Stuff"

1 (9 inch) chocolate pie crust
1 (7.25 ounce) jar chocolate fudge Magic Shell ice cream topping
1/2 gallon chocolate mint ice cream
1 (8 ounce) Cool Whip
1 (1.35 ounce) Hershey bar
chocolate sauce, drizzled

Pour magic shell topping all over pie crust, sides too.
Mix ice cream and Cool Whip together.
Pour into pie crust.
Shave chocolate bar on top.
Drizzle with chocolate sauce.
Freeze until **ready** to serve.

Pecan Pie

"Southern Blonde Lust"

- **1/2 stick margarine, softened**
- **1 cup sugar**
- **4 eggs**
- **3/4 cup light corn syrup**
- **1 1/4 cups pecan halves**
- **1 (9 inch) pie shell, unbaked**

Mix first 4 ingredients together.
Stir in pecans.
Pour filling into unbaked pie shell.
Bake at 375 degrees for 5 minutes.
Reduce heat to 325 degrees, **cook** for another 45 minutes.

Strawberry Pie

"Shameless"

- **1 (9 inch) pie shell**
- **2 cups strawberries, sliced**
- **3 Tablespoons cornstarch**
- **2 cups sugar**
- **1 (3 ounce) box strawberry jello**
- **1 cup water**

Bake pie shell according to directions.
Put strawberries in pie shell.
Mix next 4 ingredients in saucepan.
Cook until thick and clear.
Pour mixture over strawberries, **chill**.

4 Layer Dessert

"She's Stacked"

1 stick margarine, melted
1 cup self-rising flour
1 (8 ounce) cream cheese, softened
1 (12 ounce) Cool Whip
1 cup powdered sugar
2 (3 ounce) boxes instant chocolate pudding

1st Layer:
Mix margarine and flour together.
Layer in 9x13 inch dish.
2nd Layer:
Mix cream cheese, 1 cup Cool Whip, powdered sugar together.
Layer over 1st layer.
3rd Layer:
Mix pudding according to directions.
Layer over 2nd layer.
4th Layer:
Use rest of Cool Whip on 3rd layer.

Q: How can you tell if a blonde's been using the computer?
A: There's Wite-Out on the screen.

6 Layer Bars

"Lay Her"

1 stick margarine
2 cups cinnamon graham cracker crumbs
1 (12 ounce) bag chocolate chips
1 (12 ounce) bag butterscotch chips
1½ cups pecans, chopped
1 (14 ounce) can condensed milk

Combine butter and graham cracker crumbs.
Spread evenly in 9x13 dish.
Sprinkle next 3 ingredients over crumbs.
Pour condensed milk evenly over top.
Bake at 350 degrees for 35 minutes.

Almond Granola Bars

"Awe Man!"

⅓ cup margarine, melted
3 cups granola cereal
1 (6 ounce) bag chocolate chips
½ cup sliced almonds
⅓ cup coconut
1 (14 ounce) can condensed milk

Put margarine in 9x13 dish.
Sprinkle granola over melted butter.
Bake at 350 degrees for 10 minutes, cool.
Layer next 3 ingredients.
Pour condensed milk over mixture.
Bake on 350 degrees for 20-25 minutes.

Blueberry Delight

"Don't Be Blue"

1 (8 ounce) cream cheese, softened
3/4 cup sugar
1 teaspoon vanilla extract
2 eggs
1 (9 inch) graham cracker crust
1 (21 ounce) can blueberry pie filling

Mix first 4 ingredients together.
Pour mixture in pie crust.
Spread pie filling over mixture.
Chill for 4 hours before serving.

Caramel Bread Pudding

"Melt In Your Mouth"

6 biscuits or rolls
1/2 stick of margarine, melted
3 cups milk
1 (10 ounce) caramel icing
6 eggs, beaten
2 teaspoons vanilla extract

Break biscuits in melted margarine and **put** in 9x13 pan.
Mix rest of ingredients together.
Pour over biscuits.
Bake at 350 degrees for 45-50 minutes.

anotherblondemoment.com

Raisin Bread Pudding

"Smirkie Kirkie"

6 slices Cinnamon Swirl Raisin Bread, cubed
1/2 cup raisins
2 cups milk
2 eggs
1/4 cup sugar
2 teaspoons vanilla extract
1/4 teaspoon salt
1/4 teaspoon cinnamon
1/4 teaspoon nutmeg

Grease a 2 quart baking dish.
Combine bread and raisins in baking dish.
Combine rest of ingredients and blend well.
Pour over bread and raisins.
Bake at 350 degrees **uncovered** for 45-50 minutes.

Raisin Bread Pudding Sauce:

1 1/4 cups powered sugar
1 stick margarine
1 egg
1/4 cup dark rum
1/8 teaspoon vanilla extract
1/8 teaspoon cinnamon

Combine all ingredients.
Cook over low heat until thickened.
Serve over pudding.

Baby Ruth Cream Cheese Brownies

"Babe's Best"

- **1 (16 ounce) box brownie mix**
- **4 (2.1 ounce) Baby Ruth bars**
- **1 (8 ounce) cream cheese, softened**
- **1 egg**
- **1/2 cup sugar**
- **1/2 teaspoon vanilla extract**

Make brownies according to box, but don't cook.
Chop candy bars into 1/4 inch chunks.
Mix rest of ingredients in a separate bowl.
Fold in chopped candy bar.
Spread brownie mix in 9x13 pan.
Spoon cream cheese mixture on top of brownie mix.
Swirl cream cheese and brownie mix to create a swirl.
Bake at 325 degrees for 35 minutes.

Q: Why do blondes wear shoulder pads?
A: (With a rocking of the head from side to side) I dunno!

Chocolate Brownie Cup Cakes

"It's All In The Cups"

4 squares of chocolate bars
2 sticks margarine
1 teaspoon vanilla extract
1 cup plain flour
2 cups sugar
4 eggs

Melt the first 3 ingredients together in double boiler.
Mix the next 3 ingredients in separate bowl.
Combine all ingredients together and **pour** into greased muffin tins.
Bake at 325 degrees for 25 minutes.

Chess Squares

"Flat Chest"

1 stick margarine, softened
1 box yellow cake mix
4 eggs
1 (8 ounce) cream cheese, softened
1 teaspoon vanilla extract
powdered sugar

Mix margarine, cake mix, and 1 egg together until crumbly.
Press in greased 9x13 dish.
Cream 3 eggs and next 2 ingredients.
Pour over crumbled mixture.
Bake at 325 degrees for 45 minutes.
Cut into squares.
Sprinkle with powdered sugar.

Chocolate Chip Cream Cheese Bars

"Rollin' In The Dough"

2 (8 ounce) chocolate chip cookie dough rolls
1 (8 ounce) cream cheese, softened
3/4 cup sugar
1 egg
1 teaspoon vanilla extract
Pam cooking spray

Press 1 roll of cookie dough in 9x13 dish.
Mix rest of ingredients.
Spread over dough.
Spray hands with Pam.
Press other cookie dough roll over mixture.
Bake at 350 degrees for 30 minutes.

The Jumper

A blonde and a redhead met in a bar after work for a drink and were watching the six o'clock news. A man was shown threatening to jump from the Brooklyn Bridge. The blonde bet the redhead $50 he wouldn't jump, and the redhead replied, "I'll take that bet!" Anyway, sure enough he jumped, so the blonde gave the redhead the $50 she owed. The redhead said, "I can't take this, you're my friend." The blonde said, "No, a bet's a bet. You won the money." So the redhead said, "Listen, I have to admit, I saw this on the five o'clock news, so I can't take your money." The blonde replied, "Well so did I, but I never thought he'd jump again."

Coconut Chews

"Ooey Gooey"

- 1 box white cake mix
- 1 stick margarine
- 1/4 cup milk
- 1 (3 ounce) can flaked coconut
- 1 (12 ounce) jar of caramel topping
- 1/4 cup flour

Mix first 3 ingredients together until crumbly.
Set aside 1 cup of mixture.
Pat the rest of mixture down in 9x13 greased dish.
Bake at 350 degrees for 15 minutes.
Sprinkle coconut over baked crust.
Heat the caramel and flour until dissolved.
Drizzle over coconut.
Sprinkle the reserve cup of mixture.
Bake at 350 degrees for 20-25 more minutes.
Cut into squares.

Q: What do you call a brunette with a blonde on either side?
A: An interpreter

Frozen Pink Delight
"Chelly Belly"

1 (8 ounce) cream cheese, softened
3/4 cup sugar
1 (20 ounce) can crushed pineapples, drained
1 (10 ounce) frozen strawberries
2 bananas, sliced
1 (8 ounce) Cool Whip

Mix all ingredients together.
Pour into bundt pan and **freeze** until firm.
Cover with foil and **slice**.
Can also be **frozen** in muffin tins for individual servings.

German Chocolate Bars
"Naughty Naughty"

1 box German chocolate cake mix
3 eggs
1 teaspoon vanilla extract
1 stick margarine, softened
1 (8 ounce) cream cheese, softened
1 (16 ounce) box powdered sugar

Mix together cake mix, 1 egg and margarine.
Press into greased 9x13 dish.
Mix cream cheese, 2 eggs, vanilla and sugar.
Pour on top of cake mixture.
Bake at 350 degrees for 45 minutes.
Cut into squares.

Homemade Ice-Cream

"Queen's Cream"

- **$^1/_2$ gallon milk**
- **1 (14 ounce) can condensed milk**
- **1 cup sugar**
- **5 eggs**
- **1 Tablespoon vanilla extract**
- **1 pint whipping cream**

Combine all ingredients and **mix** well.
Put into electric ice cream freezer.
Freeze according to directions.

Ice Cream Sandwich Delights

"Delta Darlins' Ice"

- **8 ice cream sandwiches**
- **1 (12 ounce) jar caramel topping**
- **1 (12 ounce) Cool Whip**
- **1 (8 ounce) bag Heath Bar pieces**
- **chocolate shavings**
- **cherry on top**

Place ice cream sandwiches in 9x9 dish, arrange to fit pan.
Layer rest of ingredients in order.
Put in freezer.
Cut into squares when ready to serve.

Microwave Fudge

"Quickie"

$1^1/_2$ sticks margarine
3 cups sugar
$^2/_3$ cup evaporated milk
1 (12 ounce) bag chocolate chips
1 teaspoon vanilla extract
1 (7 ounce) jar marshmallow cream

Melt margarine in microwave for 1 minute.
Add sugar and evaporated milk.
Cook in microwave for 3 minutes.
Stir and **microwave** for 2 more minutes.
Stir and **microwave** 3 more minutes.
Stir and **microwave** for $3^1/_2$ more minutes.
Add chips and **stir** until melted.
Add marshmallow cream and vanilla.
Put in 9x13 pan.
Cut into squares.

Q: What do you call a blonde between two brunettes?
A: A mental block.

Lemon Squares

"Pucker Him Up"

- 2 sticks margarine
- 2 cups self-rising flour
- 1 cup powdered sugar
- 1/2 cup lemon juice
- 4 eggs
- 2 cups sugar

Mix first 3 ingredients, **put** in bottom of greased 9x13 dish.
Bake at 350 degrees for 20 minutes.
Beat last 3 ingredients.
Pour over crust.
Bake for 20 more minutes.
Cut into squares.

Rice Pudding

"Down & Dirty"

- 2 cups rice, cooked
- 1/2 cup raisins
- 2 cups hot milk
- 2 eggs, beaten
- 1/2 cup sugar
- 1/2 teaspoon salt
- 1 teaspoon vanilla extract
- dash of cinnamon
- dash of nutmeg

Mix all ingredients together.
Bake at 325 degrees for 1 hour.

Strawberry Delight

"Afternoon Delight"

1 stick margarine, softened
2 eggs, beaten
1 (16 ounce) box powdered sugar
1 (12 ounce) box vanilla wafers, crumbled
1 quart strawberries, sliced
1 (8 ounce) Cool Whip

Mix first 3 ingredients together.
Put in 9x9 baking dish.
Place crumbled wafers over mixture.
Slice strawberries on top of wafers.
Top with Cool Whip.

Paint Me Blonde

This blonde decides one day that she is sick and tired of all these blonde jokes and how all blondes are perceived as stupid, so she decides to show her husband that blondes really are smart.

While her husband is off at work, she decides that she is going to paint a couple of rooms in the house. The next day, right after her husband leaves for work, she gets down to the task at hand.

Her husband arrives home at 5:30 and smells the distinctive smell of paint. He walks into the living room and finds his wife lying on the floor in a pool of sweat. He notices that she is wearing a ski jacket and a fur coat at the same time.

He goes over and asks if she is OK. She replies yes.

He asks what she is doing. She replies that she wanted to prove to him that not all blonde women are dumb and she wanted to do it by painting the house.

He then asks her why she has a ski jacket over her fur coat. She replies that she was reading the directions on the paint can and they said, "FOR BEST RESULTS, PUT ON TWO COATS."

Index

Mug Shot

Three blondes were witnesses to a crime, so they went to the police station to identify the suspect. The police chief said he would show them a mug shot of someone for thirty seconds, then ask each one for a description. After showing the photo to the first blonde, he covered it, then asked her how she would recognize the suspect.

"Easy," she replied. "He only has one eye."

The police chief showed the photo to the second blonde. The second blonde responded, "He only has one ear."

"What is the matter with you people?!? It is a profile shot! You are seeing him from the side!" He repeated the procedure for the third blonde, then said, "How would you recognize the suspect? Now think before you give me a stupid answer."

After viewing the photo, she thought for a minute, then said, "He's wearing contact lenses."

This took the chief by surprise. He looked real hard at the picture and couldn't tell if the suspect had contacts or not, so he went into the database and looked at the report. Sure enough, when the mug shot was taken, he was wearing contact lenses! He went back to her and asked, "How could you tell he was wearing contact lenses? Nobody else here in this precinct saw that!"

"Well," she said, "he can't wear regular glasses with only one eye and one ear, now, can he?"

Index

A

B

C

D

E

F

G

H

I

J

K

L

M

N

O

AnotherBlondeMoment.com

Please send ______ copy(ies) @ $19.95 each__________

Postage and Handling @ $ 5.00 each__________

Mississippi residents add 7% sles tax @ $ 1.40 each__________

TOTAL __________

Name ______________________________

Address ______________________________

City ____________________ State ________ Zip __________

Make checks payable to

AnotherBlondeMoment.com
P. O. Box 320747
Flowood, MS 39232

Credit Cards accepted (check one)

________ Visa ________ MasterCard

Number:______________________ Expiration: __________

Cardholder's signature: ______________________________

Phone number:______________________________

AnotherBlondeMoment.com

Please send ______ copy(ies) @ $19.95 each__________

Postage and Handling @ $ 5.00 each__________

Mississippi residents add 7% sles tax @ $ 1.40 each__________

TOTAL __________

Name ______________________________

Address ______________________________

City ____________________ State ________ Zip __________

Make checks payable to

AnotherBlondeMoment.com
P. O. Box 320747
Flowood, MS 39232

Credit Cards accepted (check one)

________ Visa ________ MasterCard

Number:______________________ Expiration: __________

Cardholder's signature: ______________________________

Phone number:______________________________

AnotherBlondeMoment.com

Please send ______ copy(ies) @ $19.95 each__________

Postage and Handling @ $ 5.00 each__________

Mississippi residents add 7% sles tax @ $ 1.40 each__________

TOTAL __________

Name ______________________________

Address ______________________________

City ____________________ State ________ Zip __________

Make checks payable to
AnotherBlondeMoment.com
P. O. Box 320747
Flowood, MS 39232

Credit Cards accepted (check one)

________ Visa ________ MasterCard

Number:____________________ Expiration: __________

Cardholder's signature: ______________________________

Phone number:______________________________

AnotherBlondeMoment.com

Please send ______ copy(ies) @ $19.95 each__________

Postage and Handling @ $ 5.00 each__________

Mississippi residents add 7% sles tax @ $ 1.40 each__________

TOTAL __________

Name ______________________________

Address ______________________________

City ____________________ State ________ Zip __________

Make checks payable to
AnotherBlondeMoment.com
P. O. Box 320747
Flowood, MS 39232

Credit Cards accepted (check one)

________ Visa ________ MasterCard

Number:____________________ Expiration: __________

Cardholder's signature: ______________________________

Phone number:______________________________